# Oriental Images

# Oriental Images

## New Designs
## for Needlepoint and Stitchery

## Shirley Marein

A Studio Book
The Viking Press    New York

**Also by Shirley Marein**

Off the Loom: *Creating with Fibre*
Stitchery Needlepoint, Appliqué, and Patchwork: *A Complete
   Guide*
Creating Rugs and Wall Hangings: *A Complete Guide*
Flowers in Design

Designs, adaptations, needlework, and photography are by the
author except as otherwise credited in the legends to the
illustrations.

First published in 1978 by The Viking Press
625 Madison Avenue, New York, N.Y. 10022
Published simultaneously in Canada by
Penguin Books Canada Limited

Library of Congress Cataloging in Publication Data
Marein, Shirley.
   Oriental images.
   (A Studio book)
   1. Needlework—Patterns.   2. Embroidery—
Patterns.   3. Design, Decorative—Near East.
4. Design, Decorative—East Asia.   I. Title.
TT753.M35      746.4′4      78–2269
ISBN 0–670–52861–7

Text and black-and-white illustrations printed in
the United States of America. Color illustrations
printed in Japan.

# Contents

*For Joel and Aaron*

# Preface

Richly ornate, intricate Eastern design elements have flickered in and out of Western consciousness for centuries. Interest wanes periodically, particularly when national borders close for political reasons, but beauty is self-evident and emerges again and again, to be freshly discovered by each new generation. Design motifs evolved naturally from uncomplicated Neolithic sources into elaborate conventions as communications developed among the civilizations found in the valleys of the Nile, the Tigris-Euphrates, the Indus, and the Yellow rivers. Of these the Chinese culture, originally centered around the Yellow River, is the oldest enduring civilization with the widest Eastern sphere of influence.

That cultural borrowing existed is a well-known fact. Trade routes, territorial expansion, the spread of religious tenets, migrations, and the effects of enmities, power, and greed might explain the infusion of Chinese inventions such as the endless scrolls, lattice geometrics, or stylized cloud forms into an Islamic culture that eventually spread as far west as Spain and southern France. More important than historical data is the preservation and accretion of design forms and patterns for the education and use of the artist. Implicit in the pursuit of art is the attendant possibility that through assimilation the creative spirit will find new variations on these traditional themes. After all, representations of the simurgh, a giant mythical bird of Persian derivation, are but artists' adaptations of China's mythological phoenix.

# Introduction

## Materials, Equipment, and Techniques

In the course of adapting these designs for the needle arts, it became apparent that diagrammatic drawings for needlepoint, stitchery, and appliqué or patchwork are interchangeable and may be adapted for hooking rugs as well. Sometimes just a few minor adjustments are necessary; for instance, seam allowances must be added for patchwork and appliqué. A single line drawing suitable for stitchery can be used for needlepoint by placing the canvas directly over the drawing and marking the canvas with a fine felt-tip pen containing ink guaranteed not to discolor yarns. (Sanford's Nepo marker is recommended.) A design that has been previously graphed for needlepoint can be converted to a line drawing for embroidery by using the small boxes as a guide. Translate the curves into a linear stroke by running a pencil or marker diagonally through each box. Rule straight vertical and horizontal lines through the center of the boxes.

### How to Use the Diagrams Effectively

Unless otherwise stated, 10-mesh penelope canvas has been used for the needlepoint examples shown in the photographs. The graphed designs were drawn on paper measuring ten squares to the inch, but some of the diagrams are reduced in size to fit the book format. In each case the original size of the needlepoint piece is stated. The diagrams can be used directly from the book itself by counting the boxes from color area to color area, but you may find it helpful to photocopy the page or sections of the diagram for closer, easier reference. Most libraries and banks have copying machines available to the public. Do not be surprised by evidence of shrinkage in the process. It has little effect on the finished work because each box simply represents one needlepoint stitch on penelope or mono canvas of any size. One box can also represent four petit-point stitches if penelope canvas is used. A photostat enlargement, although more expensive than an ordinary photocopy, is clearer and can render the detail even more visible. Somewhat time-consuming, but worthwhile as a way of getting acquainted with the design, is copying it from the book onto a separate sheet of graph paper. Experiment with personal color choices on the graph paper, using crayons or Magic Markers. The involvement is creatively stimulating.

To convert an embroidery design (such as "Chinoiserie") to a needlepoint pattern, enlarge the design to the desired size. Lay a sheet of graph paper over the enlarged design. Fill in the boxes along the lines of the design, following the contours of the original as closely as you can. *Note:* If the squares of the graph paper are ten to the inch, the enlargement must be sufficient so that the curves will be gradual. For a complicated design with fine detail, it is advisable to use a finer grid with more squares to the inch.

## Background Materials

### Needlepoint Canvas

Both double-thread penelope and single-thread mono canvas are available in a variety of sizes for needlepoint stitches. (The mesh count number refers to the number of stitches per inch.) Ten-mesh penelope canvas was used for these examples because of its dual service. By spreading the double warp and weft threads to make the stitches, it is possible to introduce petit-point areas at any point in the design. Use a blunt needle to spread the threads. The combination of needlepoint and petit point allows for variation in texture, gradual curves, and more detail.

The designs in this book can be worked on several different mesh sizes and adapted to others. The over-all size of the given design decreases as the number of stitches per square inch increases. There is very little difference in finished size when the design is worked on 10- or 12-mesh canvas. It will be necessary to enlarge the background area or extend all four sides of the design in order to maintain the original finished size when using 14- or 16-mesh canvas. In effect the central design elements will decrease in size and appear smaller in the midst of a larger background.

### Fabrics for Embroidery

Linen, Hardanger, and Aida cloth are suitable for counted-thread embroidery because it must be worked on a clear, even-weave fabric in order to achieve a crisp geometric pattern. Scandinavia's cotton Hardanger cloth, available in white, natural, and several pastel colors, shows regular spacing of twenty intersections to the inch, easily counted and ready to receive the needle right on target without splitting threads. The surface is smooth and lovely, suitable for clothing, tablecloths, napkins, place mats, and pillows. Aida cloth has a count of ten to the inch. This soft, supple cotton cloth, available in white or beige, takes to a dye bath easily and serves as a guide for making perfect cross-stitches. The surface is ideal for training the young embroiderer, as well as for helping an experienced emboiderer whose sight is not keen.

Almost any material with a visible intersection between the crossing of the warp and the weft is suitable for counted-thread embroidery. Smooth, evenly woven linen is also commendable. Its lovely matte finish has a rich luster and a slight texture.

Silk shantung, cotton twill, and linen are good backgrounds for embroidery that does not require counting threads. Sumptuous silk shantung, the favored Chinese court fabric, is a strong, workable surface. The needle glides through the silken threads with invisible strokes. Stitching on this luxurious fabric is unquestionably pleasurable for the embroiderer. Cotton or part-polyester twills, recognizable by the diagonal patterns in the weave, also present a rich, dense, opaque surface that wears well and enhances the embroidery. Linen, too, is ideal.

### Rug Backgrounds
Monk's cloth and Duraback make heavy durable backings for hooked or embroidered rugs.

## Threads and Yarns: Choices and Calculations

For *needlepoint,* three-ply Persian yarn easily covers a 10-mesh canvas. A single strand of the three-ply Persian yarn is sufficient for 20-mesh petit point. Two strands of the three-ply Persian yarn may be suitable for 14- or 16-mesh canvas, depending upon the brand. Unquestionably some wool brands are "fatter" than others. Often one strand is quite adequate on a 16-mesh canvas. A test patch is always helpful. Cotton floss or silk embroidery thread is useful for petit point (and often more practical) because the threads are smoother. Tapestry yarn, not as varied in its uses as Persian yarn, has less texture. It makes a smoother surface when large, flat areas are to be covered, but a looser stitch is necessary for full coverage on 10-mesh canvas, and even then it may not cover adequately. Tapestry yarn is well suited to 12- or 13-mesh canvas.

Yarn calculations for needlepoint are based on the amount of yarn used to stitch one square inch. An approximate gauge for tent stitch on 10-mesh penelope canvas is one yard per square inch. Continental stitch requires a little more, half cross-stitch a little less. An addition of twenty-five per cent after the calculation is made will easily cover starting and ending and variations in technique. First measure the width and depth of the canvas. Multiply the width by the depth to find how many square inches are contained in the entire stitchery. Then calculate approximately how many square inches occur in each color area. Write these amounts on a piece of paper. Total the number of square inches of all the various colors that make up the subject matter of the design and subtract this sum from the total of the stitchery to find the number of square inches of background. Often it is a good idea to measure the background area as well, as an approximate check. Your sums do not have to be accurate, just reasonable. Many brands of yarn are sold by the ounce. One-half ounce is approximately twenty-five yards, and each square inch of stitchery equals one yard of yarn.

In *embroidery* the term "crewel" refers to a worsted yarn that also has been in use for embroidery since the Middle Ages. Plied woolen yarn for weaving and decorative embroidery was in use much before the term "crewel" became synonymous with the kind of embroidery made with it. One ply of three-ply Persian yarn can be used for crewel embroidery, as well as yarn made especially for the purpose. For a flatter, smoother finish or for use in delicately outlined images, separable or other six-strand cotton floss or perle cotton thread available in several weights is recommended. Hundreds of colors and shades of colors are available to choose from.

For *blackwork,* a style of counted-thread embroidery generally employing thread of a single color, a number of weights or thicknesses are required to vary the texture and the shade of the single color from light to dark.

To *hook rag rugs,* it is generally necessary to have six times the amount of hooking fabric as that in the specific design area to be covered. Calculate the amount of material necessary by finding the number of square inches in the given area (multiply the length by the width). Multiply this figure by six to arrive at the number of square inches of hooking material needed to cover the given area. For large areas convert this figure to square feet by dividing it by 144—the number of square inches in one square foot.

For instance, a 9″ × 8″ design area makes 72 square inches to be covered. Multiplied by six, this is 432 square inches of hooking material needed. Divide this by 144, and you find you need three square feet of fabric, or one-fifth of a yard of ordinary woolen yardage. (Most new woolen fabric is woven sixty inches—five feet—wide, so a yard contains fifteen square feet.)

## Needles

Crewel and chenille needles are sharp-pointed and are differentiated by size. Numbers 1 through 10, from large to small, are fine embroidery needles. Numbers 9 and 10 have eyes so fine as to be difficult to thread. Numbers 5, 6, and 7 are satisfactory for most fine embroidery. Chenille needles, numbered 13 through 26, are large, long-eyed needles for heavy fibers and fabrics. The largest is 13, the smallest is 26. Tapestry needles correspond in numbers to chenille needles but have blunt tips. Tapestry needles are recommended for needlepoint. The blunt tip will not snag the yarn or split the canvas. A good tapestry needle of the correct size will go through the hole of the canvas without forcing or spreading it open. A number 18 or 19 tapestry needle works well on 10-mesh canvas with three-ply Persian yarn; a number 22 or 23 is suitable for petit point, using one strand of Persian yarn. Working a multicolored needlepoint or embroidery design is pleasanter when several needles are in use, to avoid unthreading and rethreading every time a change of color is desired. A complicated color scheme might have as many as eight or ten needles in use at one time. When they are not in use, insert the threaded needles in a row in a piece of folded paper for safekeeping.

## Transferring the Design

Before transferring the design, take the time to consider your needs, your method of working, and your materials. Projects can fall into different categories: traveling projects, projects to be done while watching television, creative projects, difficult projects, or a combination of these. Expect the creative process to precede a period of busy work. Many craftsmen keep several projects going at once, each having different requirements.

For *needlepoint,* select a piece of canvas two to three inches larger, exclusive of the selvage, than the planned size of the finished piece. Working with the grain of the fabric always means keeping the selvages to the right and the left of the design. Fold masking tape around all cut edges to prevent unraveling. Try to start at a point near the center of the design, which is usually the center of the canvas. Many of the graphed designs are marked with a cross at the center starting point. This may not always be the precise center, especially in an asymmetrical design. Fold the canvas in quarters, gently creasing it to find the approximate center. Mark the center with a waterproof marker, or immediately start the needlepoint with a stitch at the intersection of the creases. Count the boxes to the next color area and stitch, or mark points along the intersections of each color with small guiding crosses. (Roll the canvas up in your hand to reach the center area.) A prime consideration in needlepoint is to minimize canvas distortion due to the pull of the stitchery. Work all over the canvas to equalize the tension. If you are willing to work one stitch at a time by using two strokes, one for entering a space and pulling the thread through and the other for bringing the needle up again, all distortion can be eliminated by stapling the canvas tautly to an artist's stretcher.

For *embroidery,* trace the design onto a piece of tracing paper. If the size is unsuitable for your purpose, have the design enlarged by a photostater directly from the book or from the tracing. Or enlarge the design by the grid system, drawing a grid of small squares over the tracing and copying the outlines from each square into those of a larger grid drawn on a separate sheet of paper.

Always work on a taut surface held firm by hoops or a stretcher. All embroidery designs in this book were worked on an artist's stretcher. The fabric was cut to fit the stretchers, with sufficient allowance all around for tacking or stapling the fabric across the top, bottom, and sides. Remember when selecting stretcher sizes that it is impossible to stitch through the fabric where it goes over the stretcher strips. In some cases the stretcher can be put directly into a picture frame upon completion of the work. If the work is intended for other purposes, such as the face of a pillow, a few inches of fabric can be saved by tacking it to the flat front surface of the stretchers rather than wrapping it over them. When stretchers are used, it is best to transfer the design after the fabric is stretched. Place a piece of cardboard under the portion of the fabric where the design is to be placed. Cut the cardboard in a size that will fit between the fabric and the stretcher and rest on the flat front surface of the stretcher. If it is necessary to support a long span of fabric, place a book on the table under the center portion of the cardboard. When the design has been transferred, remove the cardboard.

Carefully position the tracing of the design on the fabric. Hold the top edge in place with masking tape or straight pins. Slide a piece of dressmaker's transfer paper under the tracing. (Never use stenographic carbon paper for transferring.) Trace the design onto the fabric with a sharp pencil. Every so often lift the paper and check the tracing for visibility. A few misses can be filled in with a pencil if necessary. It is possible to clean some marks from the surface of fabric by gently rubbing with a clean gum eraser.

If you use an embroidery hoop, cut the fabric to the desired size, including at least three extra inches all around, depending upon the purpose of the piece. Too much excess is preferable to too little. Tape the fabric to a table or drawing board to hold it straight and taut. Trace the design onto the fabric, using dressmaker's transfer paper. Always remember to cut the fabric with the grain of the material, making certain the warp and the weft are at right angles. Place the tracing of the design on the fabric, perpendicular to the horizontal (weft) threads.

Some counted-thread work on Hardanger or Aida cloth can be worked without stretching the fabric, particularly if the piece is small and cross-stitch is used. Larger pieces incorporating a variety of stitches based on running, back, and straight stitches must be held taut for best results. Always stretch a piece designed for blackwork.

### Needlepoint Stitches

Eastern design is complex, enhanced by brilliant color. Even the smallest areas are intricately conceived, so it is sensible to execute the designs in stitches that are not competitive. Most of the needlepoint examples in this book have been worked in a combination of half cross-stitch, continental stitch, and basket-weave stitch. All these stitches have the same surface appearance, but each one is suited to the needs of different parts of the design. Undoubtedly using one stitch throughout will produce the smoothest finish, but this is not always the practical thing to do. Rising diagonally, basket weave produces the least amount of pull on the canvas, minimizing distortion and the attendant need for rigorous blocking. It is strongly recommended for large background areas. Both half cross-stitch and continental stitch are used for delineating form and filling small and narrow areas.

*Half cross-stitch* is just that, one half of a cross-stitch. Working from left to right, bring the needle up in a space, cross diagonally upward over one mesh intersection, and insert the needle in the next space of the row above. Bring the needle up again in the space directly below and repeat the small diagonal stitch. The half cross-stitch is always worked from left to right, so on the return row it is necessary to turn the canvas upside down to continue working the half cross-stitch with the same

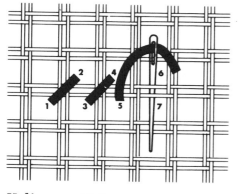

*Half cross-stitch*

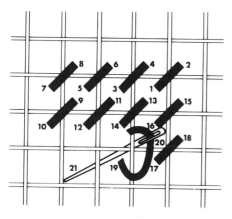

*Continental stitch*

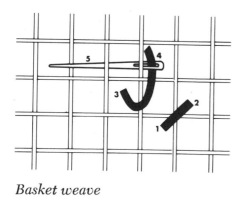

*Basket weave*

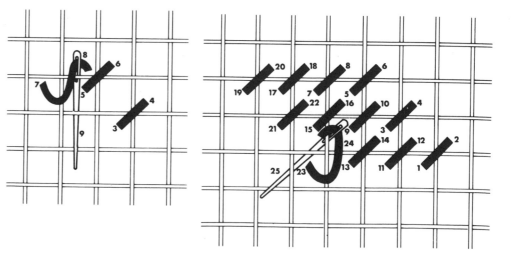

thread. In small areas it may be advantageous to work the return row with the *continental stitch*. Working from right to left, one almost automatically starts the next stitch by bringing the needle up in the space to the left of the starting insertion. Continental stitch fully covers the back of the fabric, requiring twice as much yarn as the half cross-stitch. The surface difference is barely perceptible, and the combination of the two stitches modifies the intensity of the pull inherent in the continental stitch. Both half cross-stitch and the continental stitch are used for outlining forms and filling small areas.

*Basket weave* does not have to be turned upside down to start succeeding rows. Contrary to popular belief, basket weave can be started anywhere on the canvas. Proceed diagonally upward, bringing the needle in and out horizontally for each new stitch. Bring the needle in and out vertically for the return downward, placing a stitch between two stitches from the previous row. Once the upward diagonal row is begun, each stitch will start in an empty space and finish in a filled space.

*Cross-stitch,* in either embroidery or canvas work, is slanted to the right and then to the left over one intersection, or can be doubled in size by crossing two intersections. Complete stitches individually or work in a row of half cross-stitches, completing the second half of the stitch by returning to the start of the row. Crossing all stitches in the same direction achieves surface uniformity.

Add seedlike texture to the center of exotic flowers with a variation on the cross-stitch called the *rice stitch*. Make a double-sized cross stitch over two intersections, then topstitch each corner with a short diagonal stitch in a contrasting color or one of another value. Use a single strand for the short diagonal stitch.

*Mosaic stitches* are composite variations on the long and short half cross-stitch. These units of stitches fill a wider area more rapidly than half cross-stitch. They are useful for borders, as a change of background texture, and as an accent within forms. The stitch consists of one half cross-stitch, one longer stitch made over two intersections, and then one more half cross-stitch to complete a square. Each unit can be worked horizontally, vertically, or diagonally. *Horizontal mosaic stitches* produce the most pull on the canvas, but plying the needle up and down

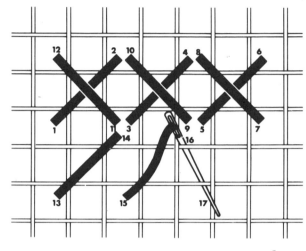

*Cross-stitch*

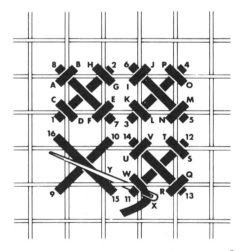

*Rice stitch*

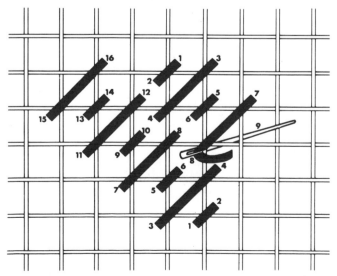

*Diagonal mosaic stitch*

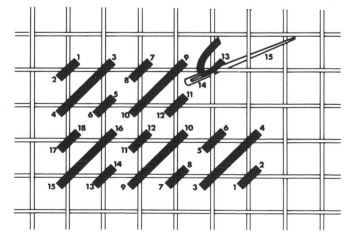

*Horizontal mosaic stitch*

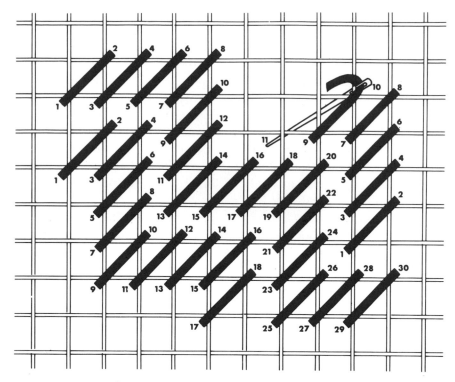

*Byzantine stitch*

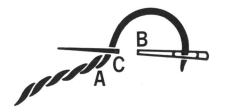

*Backstitch*

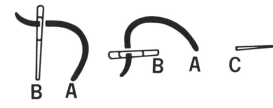

*Stem stitch*

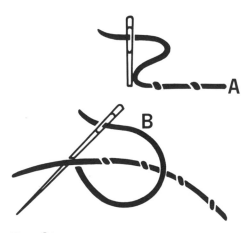

*Couching*

in single strokes will lessen the tension. Another variation is the cashmere stitch, composed of one short stitch, two long stitches, and one short stitch, forming an oblong instead of a square.

Scotch stitch, sometimes called the checkerboard stitch, is a third variation on the mosaic stitch. The first stitch is over one mesh intersection, the second over two intersections, the third over three intersections, the fourth over two, and the fifth over one mesh intersection, completing a square. Alternating rows can be stitched in a change of color or a change of stitch. Try the tent stitch between squares.

There are several variations on the *Byzantine stitch,* a diagonal zigzag stitch. Start at the upper left side for a diagonal row slanting to the right, or the upper right side for one slanting to the left. Work over two mesh intersections, completing four, five, or six slanted stitches horizontally and then an equal number vertically. Continue the zigzag until the row is complete. All subsequent rows can be filled in to fit the starting row, working up or down the zigzag. Rows can butt each other or be separated by a single row of tent stitches. Contrasting colors or tints and tones of the same color form other variations.

The straight Gobelin stitch is a simple vertical stitch taken over two or three weft threads or made in a series of graduated lengths. (Bargello stitches are similar, generally done over four and under two threads, advancing up and down by making each stitch two spaces above or below the previous one.)

**Embroidery Stitches**

Linear blackwork designs are defined by ordinary sewing stitches —the straight, running, and back stitches. Most important is *backstitch,* for outlining with precision. Outlines can also be worked in *stem stitch* or a raised outline produced by *couching* thread to the surface. Blackwork may be enriched with gold thread which is often couched to the surface. Solids are filled with *satin stitches*. These straight parallel stitches are set close together. Do not pull straight stitches too tightly.

In crewel embroidery more effective outlining is firmly controlled by the unique holding quality of *split stitch*. With the fabric under tension in a hoop or frame, make a straight stitch about ¼ inch long. Bring the needle up from underneath the fabric, splitting the yarn on the surface with the point. Draw the thread through and advance to the next stitch. *Chain stitch,* as well as split stitch, is characteristic of the earliest Chinese embroideries. With the least amount of waste on the back and the fullest surface coverage, chain stitch is used in Oriental embroidery as a filler for all curvilinear forms where movement is ongoing, either as fluffy clouds or sea foam. Bring needle and thread up through the fabric. Hold the thread on the surface to one side with your thumb while making a loop to the right. Insert the needle downward very close to the point where it emerged from the fabric. Bring the point out a short distance straight ahead. Pull the needle out over the loop. Repeat, starting the next stitch inside the previous loop. Small stitches are necessary to follow a spiraling line. Place each row close to the next. A single unit of the chain stitch is called *petal stitch*.

Tiny *French knots* produce a knurled surface highly prized by the Chinese for imitating the appearance of tightly compacted peonies and chrysanthemums just beginning to emerge but not yet in full bloom. Keep the fabric taut. Bring the needle and thread to the surface. Wind the thread once, twice, three, or more times around the needle, according to the desired size of the knot. Insert the needle point close to the starting point but not in the same hole. Pull the thread firmly to one side when the needle is partway down. Slide the knot down the needle to the surface of the fabric. Push the needle slowly through the knot and on to the underside of the fabric. Pull the thread down through the center of the knot.

## Appliqué and Patchwork

Basic basting and hemming stitches, hand- or machine-sewn, are all that is needed for appliqué and patchwork. *Appliqué* is the stitching of selected cut forms to a fabric background. Cotton fabrics are easiest to work with because the seam allowance turns under crisply and will stay in place with a minimum of trouble. Appliqué shapes without seam allowances may be zigzag stitched

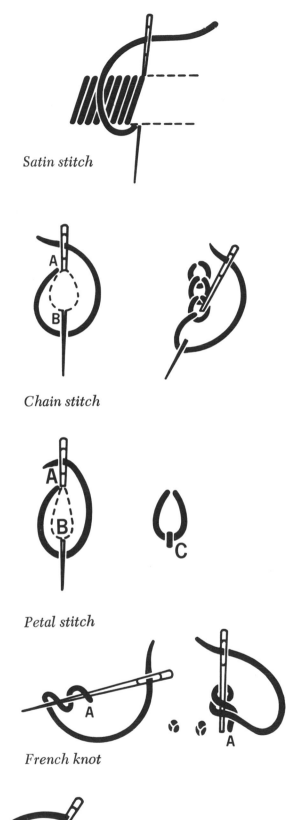

*Satin stitch*

*Chain stitch*

*Petal stitch*

*French knot*

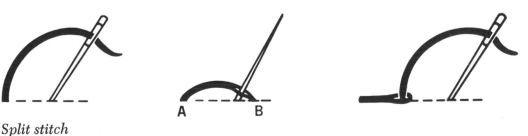

*Split stitch*

on the sewing machine or, if felt is used, blind-stitched (invisibly hemmed) to the surface. In all cases arrange the appliqué pieces in position, then pin and baste them before proceeding.

*Patchwork* is a mosaic of perfectly fitted fabric pieces arranged and stitched together to form a new entity. In order to cut perfectly sized and shaped patchwork pieces, a guide called a template is necessary. Each distinctly different form used in a patchwork design must be traced and cut out of a piece of cardboard. Like a section of a dress pattern, the cardboard form is the template from which all other like sections of the design are traced and cut from the fabric. For complete accuracy, use two templates, one in the actual finished size of the piece, and the other with an addition of a ¼-inch seam allowance. Choose fabrics of similar fibers and weaves, without a tendency to unravel, if you want an over-all uniformity of appearance. Trace around the larger template and cut out the fabric piece. Several pieces can be cut at once, but the fabric may shift if too many layers are cut at one time. Center the smaller template on the reverse side of the fabric with care. Trace a guideline for sewing. Pin the seam allowance guideline to the seam allowance of the adjoining piece and baste the two pieces before hand- or machine-sewing them together. For more exacting patchwork, fold and baste all seam allowances on each piece individually, and then, with right sides facing each other, join the patchwork pieces by overcasting the edges with fine thread of a matching color. Show as little stitchery as possible on the right side. Take special care that all points come together neatly. Pinning, adjusting the seam allowances, and basting adjoining pieces may be necessary before final sewing. Patchwork pillows, quilts, blanket covers, clothing, table accessories, or wall hangings are often padded and backed with a plain fabric. Keep padding from shifting with simple quilting, using a running stitch around each form or across larger areas. Padding can also be held in place by drawing matching or contrasting embroidery thread through the layers of fabric at regular intervals and tying a knot close to the surface to secure the long ends.

### Finishing Notes

#### Needlepoint

Needlepoint *pillows* require at least two additional rows of stitches beyond the actual finished area to provide a turn allowance before they are seamed. Needlepoint *pictures* may require five or more additional rows, depending upon the method of framing to be used. To determine how many extra rows may be needed, consult your stitchcraft shop, framer, or upholsterer (especially in the case of an upholstered chair seat) for finished size requirements. Allow for at least two inches of unworked, blank canvas all around to tack down for blocking.

If cleaning is required, it is best to have it done by an expert. You can wash needlepoint by lightly sponging the surface or immersing it briefly in cold water and a mild detergent such as Woolite, then drying it immediately with a soft towel before blocking, but this is always risky. The stiffness may be gone from the canvas, and there may be uneven shrinkage. When you have put a great deal of time and effort into stitching an intricate design, it is worth the additional investment to have it professionally dry-cleaned.

*Blocking:* If your needlepoint pillow is to be professionally finished, the upholsterer will take care of the blocking. If you block it yourself, select a board that will easily receive thumbtacks, staples, or carpet tacks. Draw the desired finished size on the board, extending lines outward at the corners so they can be seen beyond the blank canvas. Place the needlepoint face down to fit the marked size. Use thumbtacks to facilitate easy adjustment at the start, alternating from side to side. A light misting with a plant mister will soften a resistant canvas. Pull the canvas firmly into place and tack or staple it every two inches. Dampen it thoroughly with the mister and allow it to dry in place. It may be necessary to block a distorted canvas in two stages.

### Embroidery

Embroidery worked on an artist's stretcher will remain clean and pressed if four short cotton slip covers are placed over the sides of the stretched fabric background. Embroidery tacked to a stretcher generally can be placed directly into a frame. A transparent fabric may benefit if it is removed from the stretcher after sewing and mat board of a suitable color is inserted behind the embroidery before it is replaced.

Embroidery worked in hoops may need cleaning and will surely need pressing. Preserve the raised texture of the stitches by pressing gently with the embroidery face down on a bath towel.

*Note:* Most of the needlepoint examples shown in color were worked in several different brands of three-ply Persian yarn. The color numbers given with some of the more intricate designs are based on the Paternayan Brothers Color Card for Paterna Persian yarn, as a convenient means of identifying the shades used. In other needlepoint examples and in some of the embroidery examples, the type of yarns or threads used is explained in the pattern instructions for the benefit of those who may wish to duplicate the designs in the shades shown in the color plates. In all cases, of course, the patterns may be worked in any yarns and colors of the reader's choice.

Limitations of the page size have made it necessary to show some of the needlepoint patterns in sections. The gray shaded areas show where one section overlaps the other. In copying the designs to make a working pattern, eliminate the gray shaded areas and bring together the unshaded portions of the graphs.

# China

Symbolism in Chinese art is as various and as diverse in meaning as the hundreds of characters needed for precise expression in the Chinese language. In a country where, paleontologists tell us, human beings lived and developed for more than half a million years, legends and their attendant symbols are bound to proliferate. During the Chinese dynasties and even before recorded history, legends underwent continuous redefinition and were often reinterpreted. One idea was constant, however—the understanding of the forces of nature. Agriculture then, as today, had its fundamental needs and discouraging adversaries. The sun and the soil, the wind and the rain, drought and disease demanded respect. An Easterner recognizes man's relative position in the cosmic order. He feels neither superior nor inferior to other forms of life; each has its value and its place in the natural rhythm of the universe. An equitable balance is achieved through calm acceptance and homage through ritual.

Sometimes it is hard to believe that vast, dry sections of China were at one time warm, wet, and sufficiently verdant to support lions and tigers, elephants and rhinoceroses. Tigers, for instance, are symbols of strength, courage, and cunning, but they also represent fire, heat, and wind in order to balance the attributes of the mythical dragon, symbol of rivers and mists. Myth and reality are so tightly woven in the arts of China that one cannot be certain the phoenix and the chimera never existed. Breathing fire, eyes bulging, the chimera is composed of disparate parts: a lion's head, goat's body, and serpent's tail, and functions as a guardian angel, fierce but protective. Create an equitable balance, place a ferocious guardian angel between heaven and earth and the sea and, having covered all eventualities, you will be safe. Immortality is another theme, represented by Taoist symbolic figures and accompanying emblems such as the peach, the pine tree, and the crane. Eternal life naturally springs from a rock. Children in Chinese art are more often a symbol of fertility and immortality rather than simply genre art.

*Design of chrysanthemum in contemporary Chinese satin-stitch embroidery on peach silk. Courtesy of Jan Silberstein.*

*Detail of an antique mandarin costume. Collection of Belle Kicinski.*

# Chimera

(Plate 1)
Needlepoint
18½″ × 19″. Seamed pillow: 18″ × 18½″
365 square inches

*Mandarin square denoting military rank. Silk, metal, and peacock feather threads on silk satin. Early Ch'ing Dynasty (1644–1912). The Metropolitan Museum of Art, anonymous gift, 1943.*

A fierce expression is necessary for a fire-breathing lion who serves as a guarantee of protection against evil spirits. In Chinese symbolism the intrepid chimera is revered and respected, a treasure to be presented beneath a cloud of happiness, surrounded by the staunchness of rock forms and the fecundity of the sea. For the example shown in Plate 1, the following shades were used:

**Top third (sky)**
Light aqua 354, ¼ oz.
Light blue 395, ¼ oz.
Medium soft green 546, ¼ oz.
Dark soft green 530, ¼ oz.
Emerald 524, ¼ oz.
Dark grey-violet 117, 5 ozs.

**Middle third (figures)**
Cream white 015, 2 strands
Pale sienna 426, ½ oz.
Medium sienna 416, ¼ oz.
Burnt sienna 269, ¼ oz.
Dark rose 250, ¼ oz.
Red-orange 843, ¼ oz.
Medium wine 223, ¼ oz.
Deep wine 201, 3 strands

**Lower third (sea and flora)**
Dark blue-violet 611, 5 strands
Medium yellow-green 555, ¼ oz.
Light yellow-green 570, ¼ oz.
Pale yellow-green 575, ¼ oz.
Medium green 510, ¼ oz.
Dark green 505, ¼ oz.
Medium blue 385, ¼ oz.
Pale grey 186, 5 strands
Medium grey 182, ¼ oz.
Light earth 563, 5 strands
Medium earth 134, ¼ oz.
Dark earth 124, 5 strands
Mustard 433, 5 strands

25

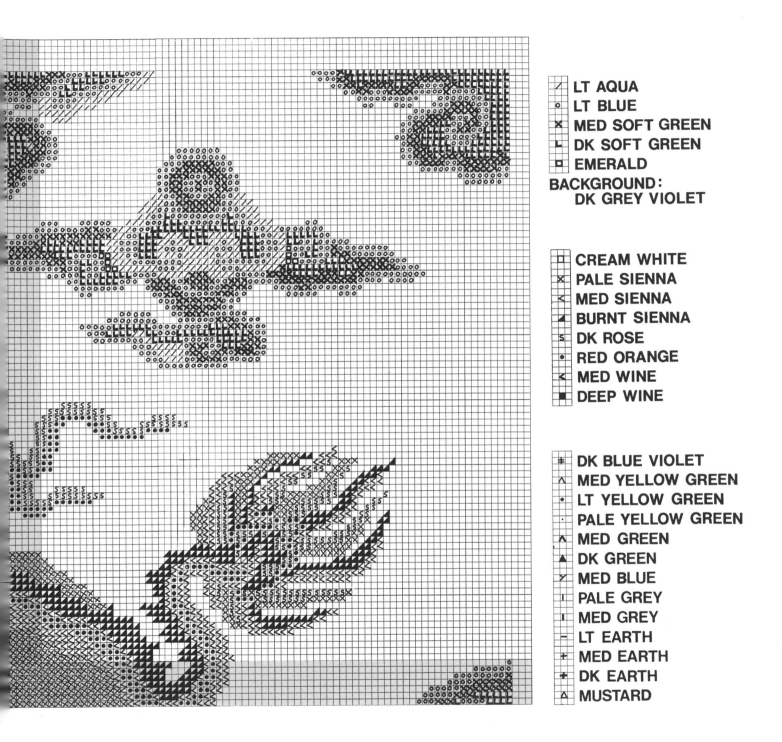

/  LT AQUA
o  LT BLUE
✗  MED SOFT GREEN
∟  DK SOFT GREEN
▫  EMERALD
BACKGROUND:
   DK GREY VIOLET


⊞  CREAM WHITE
✕  PALE SIENNA
◄  MED SIENNA
◢  BURNT SIENNA
S  DK ROSE
•  RED ORANGE
◄  MED WINE
■  DEEP WINE


⊞  DK BLUE VIOLET
∧  MED YELLOW GREEN
•  LT YELLOW GREEN
·  PALE YELLOW GREEN
∧  MED GREEN
▲  DK GREEN
⋎  MED BLUE
∥  PALE GREY
∥  MED GREY
=  LT EARTH
+  MED EARTH
+  DK EARTH
△  MUSTARD

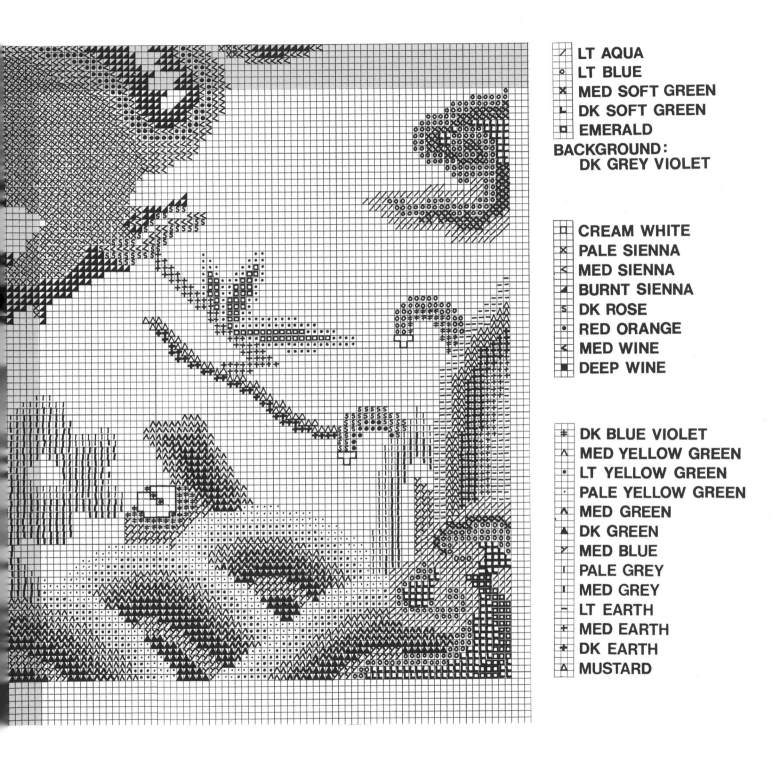

/ LT AQUA
o LT BLUE
x MED SOFT GREEN
L DK SOFT GREEN
□ EMERALD
BACKGROUND:
  DK GREY VIOLET

□ CREAM WHITE
x PALE SIENNA
< MED SIENNA
◢ BURNT SIENNA
S DK ROSE
• RED ORANGE
< MED WINE
■ DEEP WINE

+ DK BLUE VIOLET
∧ MED YELLOW GREEN
• LT YELLOW GREEN
· PALE YELLOW GREEN
∧ MED GREEN
▲ DK GREEN
⅄ MED BLUE
I PALE GREY
I MED GREY
- LT EARTH
+ MED EARTH
+ DK EARTH
∆ MUSTARD

29

# Boy Riding Ch'i-lin

(Plate 2)
Needlepoint
16¾" × 14½"
243 square inches

*"Boy Riding Ch'i-lin." Chinese em-*
*broidery of silk and gold on white*
*satin. Late eighteenth–early nineteenth*
*century. The Metropolitan Museum of*
*Art, anonymous gift, 1946.*

The fabulous creature Ch'i-lin is the Mandarin symbol for the Imperial son-in-law. The little boy riding Ch'i-lin may signify an Imperial wish for a grandson. The background colors of this piece are the several shades of celadon, a translucent pale grey-green pottery glaze. Surround the cartouche with a background done in a change of stitch, but take care that the tension is equalized. Alternate the position of the tight stitches. As the diagram shows, mosaic, cashmere, Scotch, and Byzantine stitch are suggested to add textural interest to this design.

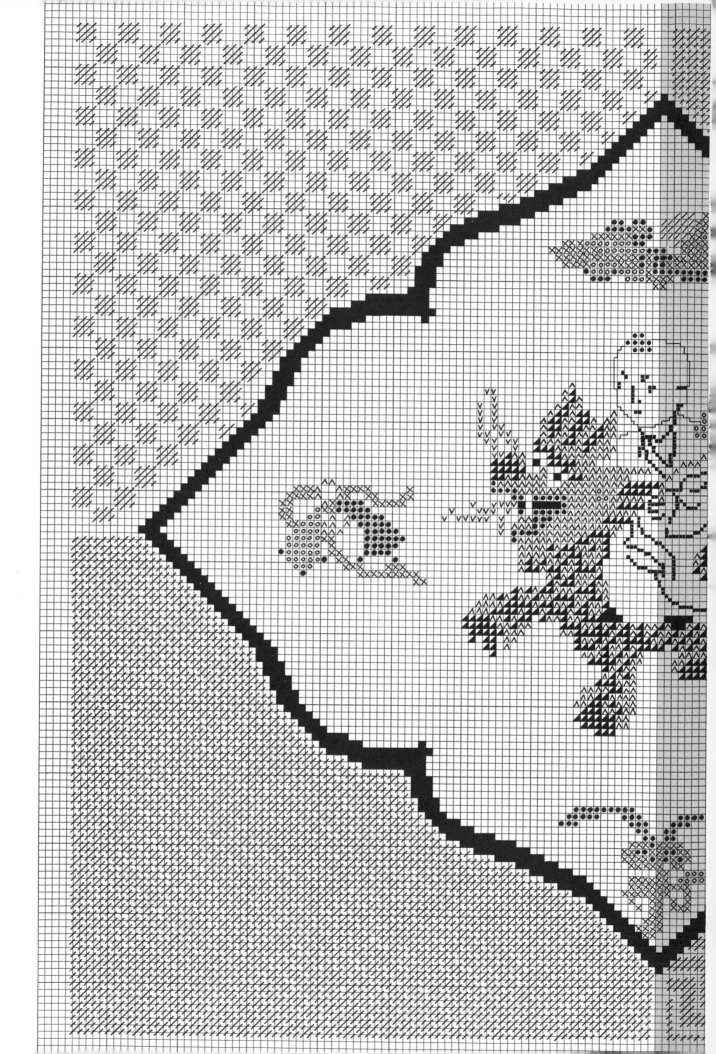

# Children at Play

(Plate 3)
Needlepoint
17" × 14½"
Area of oval is 190 square inches; area of the square, 247 square inches

*"Children at Play." K'o-ssu silk tapestry. Ming Dynasty (1368–1644). The Metropolitan Museum of Art, Fletcher Fund, 1936.*

Capture the bubbling effervescence of playful children in bright, warm, happy colors. These five sturdy little boys are probably related to the "hundred sons" theme, an antiquated Chinese point of view that envisions many sons, up to one hundred, to bring joy and support and insure the perpetuation of the family name and the preservation of its properties.

The design can be completed as an oval or as the centerpiece of a square. Shades used in the example shown in color are:

**Figures**
Black 105, ½ oz.
Dark blue 334, 5 strands
Cobalt blue 752, ¼ oz.
Off-white 020, ¼ oz.
Leaf green 553, ¼ oz.
Aqua 352, 5 strands
Dark mustard 433, ¼ oz.
Light mustard 531, 1 strand
Dark green 540, ¼ oz.
Orange 960, 5 strands
Gold 427, 5 strands

**Blossoms, tree, and background**
Pale rose 831, ¼ oz.
Medium rose 288, ¼ oz.
Dark rose 282, 7 strands
Light rose 254, ¼ oz.
Old rose 250, 5 strands
Burgundy 236, 3 oz.
Cherry red R74, 2½ oz.

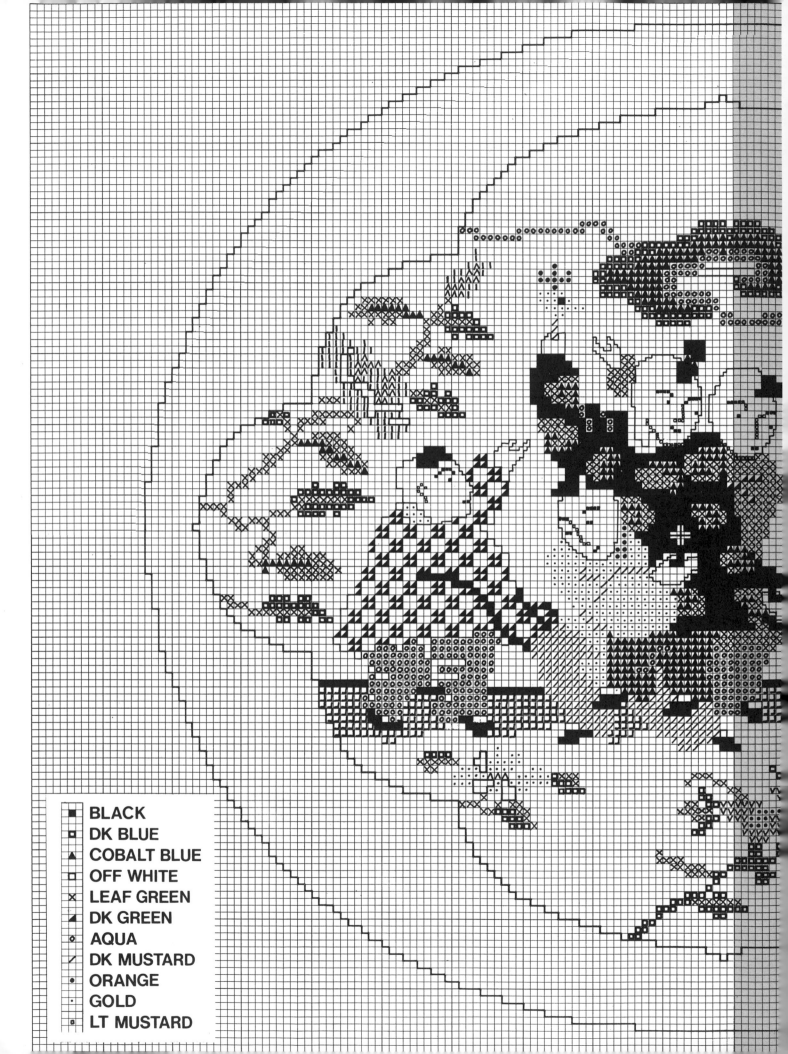

BLACK
DK BLUE
COBALT BLUE
OFF WHITE
LEAF GREEN
DK GREEN
AQUA
DK MUSTARD
ORANGE
GOLD
LT MUSTARD

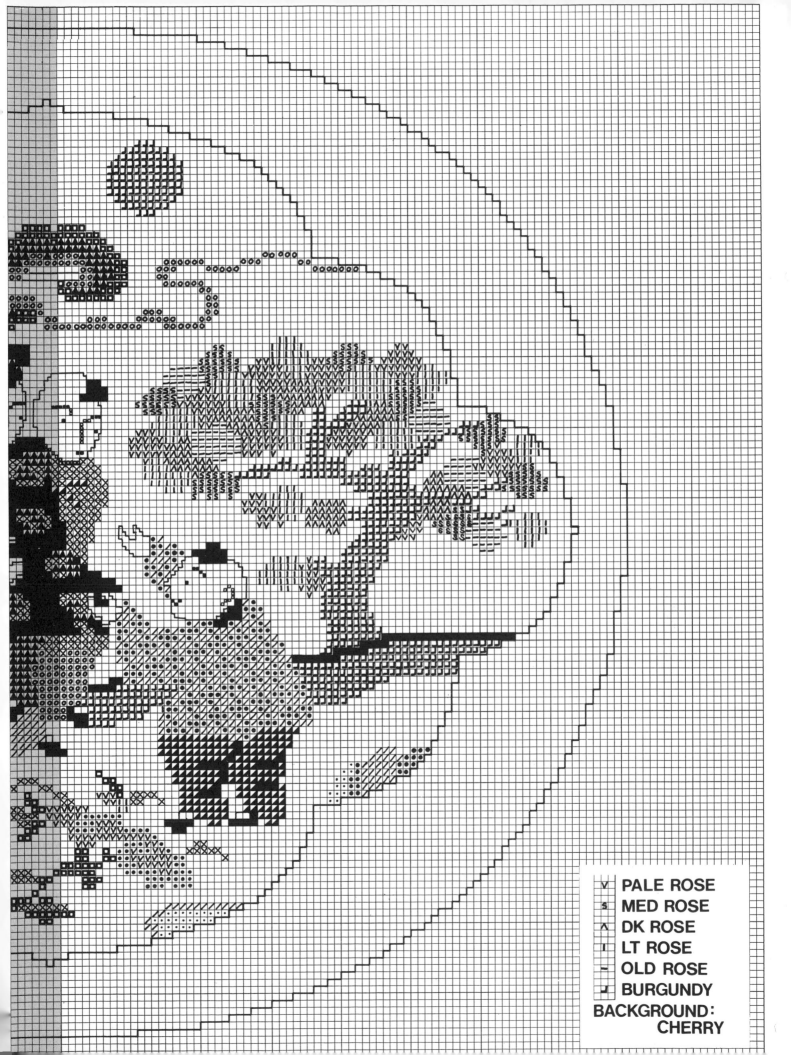

V PALE ROSE
S MED ROSE
∧ DK ROSE
I LT ROSE
— OLD ROSE
⌐ BURGUNDY
BACKGROUND:
  CHERRY

# Immortality

(Plate 4)
Embroidery
15½″ × 14½″

The polarity of Yang and Yin, expressions of the opposing forces of nature, is present in all things between heaven, the earth, and the sea. The crane, personification of supernatural longevity, is surrounded by symbols of happiness—the clouds and the bats—and by the treasured shape and substance of the eternal rocks. Sexual attainments are suggested by the soft, deeply clefted peach and the delicately cupped peony.

This is a graduate project for a master embroiderer. The stitches are petal, chain, split stitch, satin stitch, and French knots. The finished example in Plate 4 was embroidered on silk shantung with silver rayon floss and many colors of DMC cotton floss in a succession of shades from light to dark as follows:

**Top cloud bands** (blue)
Light blue 800
Medium blue 809
Dark blue 797

**Lower cloud bands** (darker blue)
Medium blue 809
Dark medium blue 322
Dark blue 311

**Crane**
Body: light grey 762; light gold 834
Legs and beak: gold 783
Eye: rust 781, brown 3031

**Peaches**
Peach-pink 951 (light); 754, 353, 352
    (dark)

**Peach tree**
Ochre 680

**Bats**
Dark red 918
Gold 783
Pink 352

**Lavender Flower**
Light violet 211
Dark violet 553

*Civil rank badge. Painted gold and polychrome silk k'o-ssu tapestry. Mid-late eighteenth century. The Metropolitan Museum of Art, anonymous gift, 1946.*

**Daffodil**
Yellow 743
Pink 352

**Peonies**
Light pink 225
Dark pink 3354

**Orange flower**
Orange 741
Rust 781

**Leaves**
Light grey-green 3053
Mustard 833
Medium yellow-green 581
Khaki 3011

**Lichen**
Medium grey-green 3052
Dull dark green 935

**Rocks**
Warm and cool greys 3024, 648,
    415, 647, 451, 413 (light to dark)

Browns—Tan 644, Earth 611,
    Sienna 433, Dark khaki 3031
Dull rose 316

**Buoys**
Aqua 993
Yellow-green 906
Emerald 912
Dark blue 820
Bright dark pink 335
Yellow 444

**Diagonal waves**
Light grey-green 928
Medium grey-green 502
Dark blue-grey 930

**Rolling waves**
Medium turquoise 598
Dark turquoise 807
Darkest turquoise 806

**Fingered waves** (light)
Pale turquoise 747
Medium turquoise 598

**Fingered waves** (dark)
Medium turquoise 598
Deep turquoise 597

**Foam**
Pale turquoise 747
Medium turquoise 598
Medium grey-green 927

**Moon**
Marlitt Cus rayon floss silver 845

*Fantail*

*Antelope*

*Flower*

## Three Mandarin Squares: Fantail, Antelope, and Flower

Embroidery

A mandarin square is a badge of social status or civil rank. These designs have been adapted from three Chinese examples made with gold thread couched in place with very fine red silk thread. Black areas on the diagrams indicate the background fabric. The white areas are reserved for couching. The shaded areas are embroidered. Graduate the color values by using long and short stitches and fine silk thread in subtle colors. Fibers such as wool yarn may be used in place of gold thread. Stitchcraft shops carry many different gold and silver-colored threads of various fibers, both shiny and matte.

Consider combining appliqué and stitchery for these designs, or duplicate the units, placing one next to the other for a block quilt. The center cartouche of both the flower and the fantail fish can be filled with initials or other designs of your choice. These squares may be enlarged or reduced in size.

41

# Good Luck

Embroidery, appliqué, or needlepoint

*The full "Good Luck" design. Use the grid to transfer the design and adjust its dimensions.*

The central motif in this design is a symbol for good luck. It is surrounded by four bats, figures that represent happiness. The grid placed over the design provides a method for reducing or enlarging the design. The design area has been closely boxed with a diagonal from corner to corner, and the interior space evenly divided. A vertical line dropped from any point on the diagonal extending beyond the enclosed area to the horizontal line at the base of the enclosure will increase the size of the drawing in proportion. Any line dropped from the diagonal within the enclosure will reduce the design. Draw the new dimension on another piece of paper and divide the interior space, duplicating the number of squares on the original drawing. Transfer the design from square to square. This design was transferred to tracing paper first, then transparent graph paper was placed over the tracing to form a needlepoint grid. Only one bat is shown in the grid as the design is symmetrical and the three others may be copied and centered on the remaining sides.

*A quarter section of "Good Luck" graphed for needlepoint.*

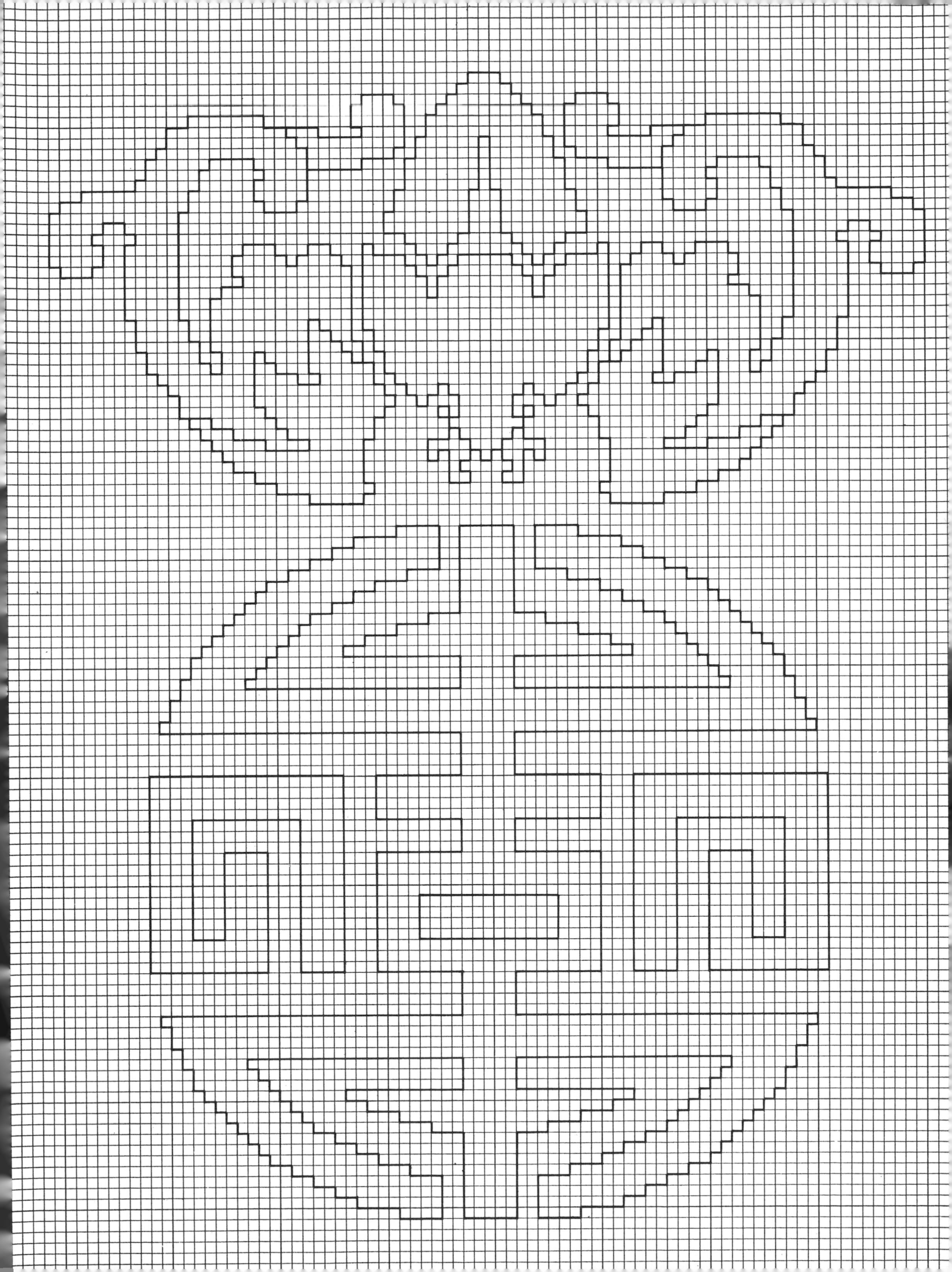

# Chinoiserie

Needlepoint or stitchery

Westernization of Chinese art occurred during the eighteenth century as the court artists tried to master the realistic contours of European art by using shading and perspective. Some of the atmospheric, emotional content in landscape was relinquished for more

formal decoration, particularly in export
porcelains. *"Chinoiserie"* was adapted
from a porcelain barrel-shaped garden
seat on which the design appeared
in blue shading on a white ground with
small touches of red.

A detail of "Chinoiserie" graphed for needlepoint. To make a needlepoint or stitchery pattern for the entire design, follow directions given under the heading "How to use the diagrams effectively" in the Introduction.

In the finished example, this traditional Cloud Band design has been worked in shades of blue on an insert of needlepoint canvas in a denim sun hat. It might be used for many purposes—as a panel to decorate a pocket, a repeat pattern for a skirt border, or arranged in various ways, either alone or with other design elements, to form an all-over pattern.

*Contemporary American sun hat with needlepoint insert.*

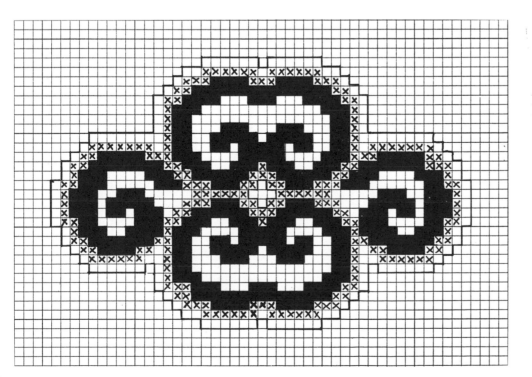

*Design of birds on a Japanese lacquered box. Collection of Melissa and Michael Cornfeld.*

# Japan

Millenniums away in the far, far distant past Japan was linked to the Asian continent by a land bridge. Even after the islands were separated, Chinese and Korean contacts formed the main prehistoric influences on Japanese culture. The techniques for making bronze and working with iron and other metals were introduced from China. Japanese craftsmen during the earlier hunting and fishing primitive Jomon era created functional earthenware with running linear and spiraling patterns on impressed or raised surfaces. Later the bases for orderly geometric constructions known as latticework were derived from the calligraphic inscriptions and ornamentation on China's Shang bronzes, and from the simple patterning of intersecting lines observed on the robes of Buddhist priests. These decorative motifs include single and composite arrangements of triangles, diamonds, zigzags, circles both plain and concentric, spirals, and multiple leafy frond forms. Concentric arcs and complex arrangements of closed and open-ended triangles were most frequently used. With the advent of Buddhism, again from the Asian continent via its original sources in India, motifs literally flowered. A palmette of fluid leaves and tendrils (known as the honeysuckle motif, but strongly suspected of having been derived from the wild hemp plant common to the entire Orient) appears individually and with the lotus blossom. Conventionalized peonies and chrysanthemums serve as the basis for patterning on almost every decorative art form, reaching the ultimate in decorative design for the hereditary crests of Japanese families.

Japanese design is an integral part of Japanese life. Beautiful objects, clothing, and personal surroundings are functional, providing an atmosphere of calm serenity for these innately tasteful people. Shibori, the art of tie dyeing on cotton fabric, is a folk technique using indigo, a dark blue natural colorant. These simple geometric dot designs in contrasting blue and white evolved into richer patterning with the advent of the advanced technique of stencil cutting for quicker production. Now, adapted to stitchery using coarse white thread on a dark ground, the single color simplicity is a gentle reminder of a rapidly vanishing art.

*Expressions of love are a rewarding subject for stitchery.*

# Love

(Plate 5)
Needlepoint
14⅜″ diameter (finished size about 14″)
171 square inches

*The Japanese ideogram for love.*

In Japanese the ideogram for the word "love" is as beautiful as the sentiment. Set off the rich black lettering with a neutral cocoa background. Brighten the surrounding area with veined leaves in strong blue and green. The needlepoint design is divided into three concentric rings. A slightly darker tan is used on the center ring to provide a stopping point and a division for the movement of the leaves.

Green 532, ¾ oz.
Blue 330, 1¼ oz.
Yellow (beige) 455, ¼ oz.
Black 050, ¼ oz.
Tan (cocoa) 257, 1½ oz.
Slightly darker tan 249, ½ oz.

53

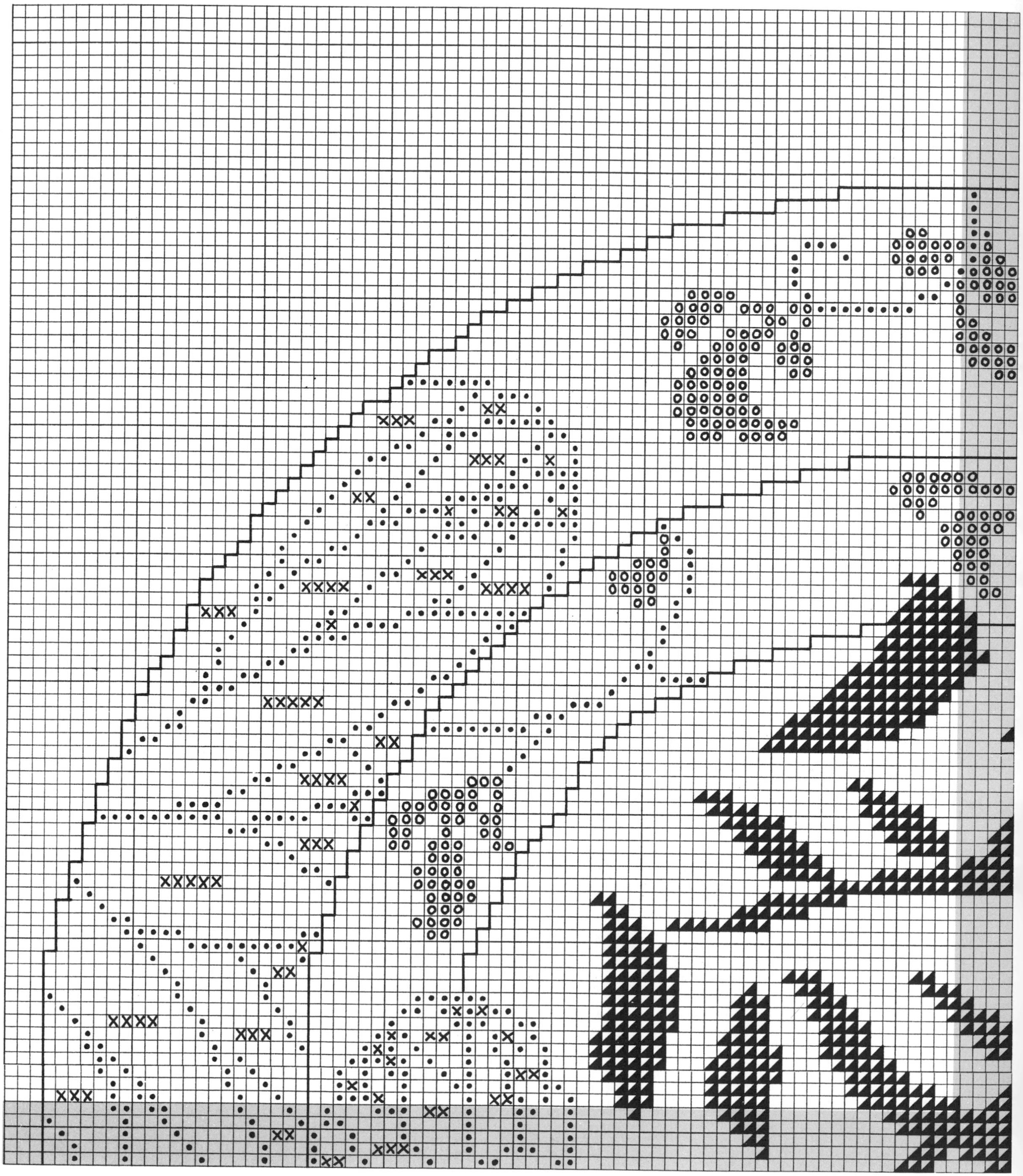

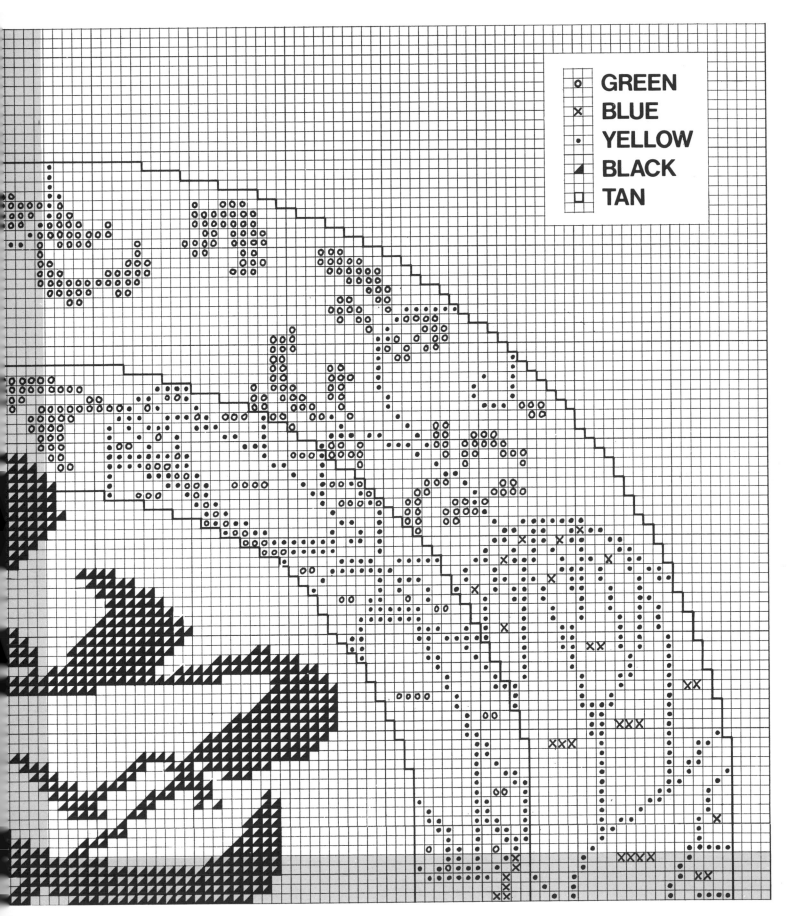

GREEN
BLUE
YELLOW
BLACK
TAN

55

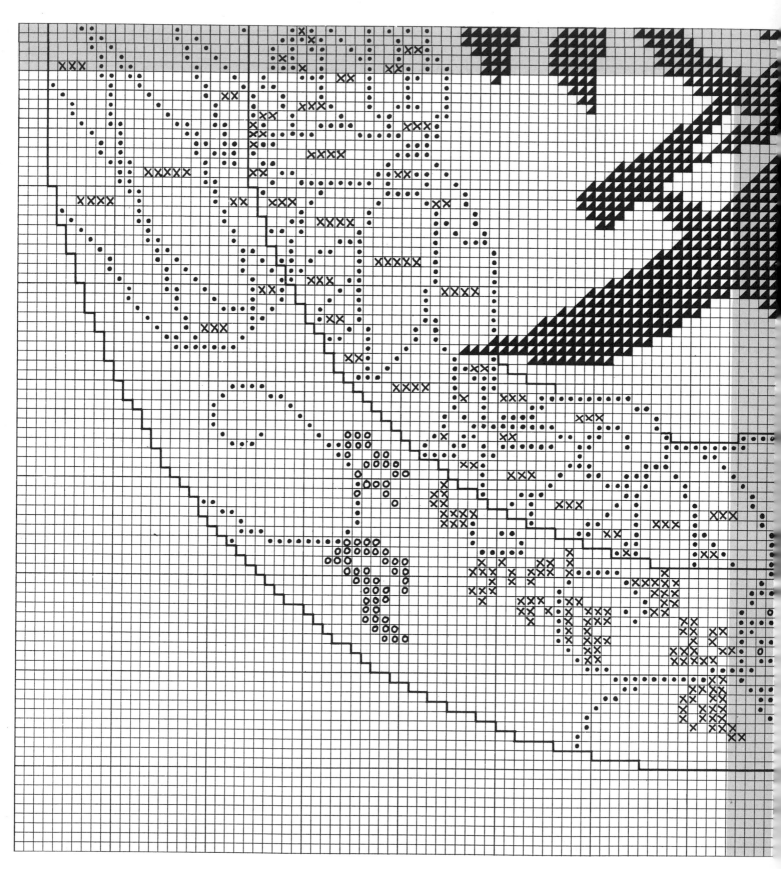

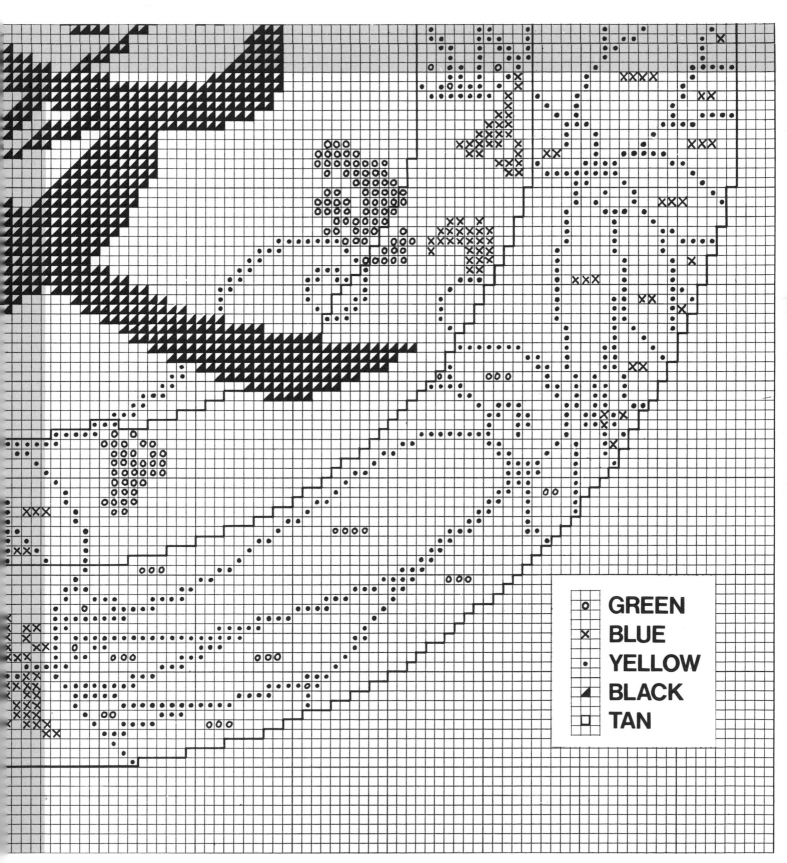

GREEN
BLUE
YELLOW
BLACK
TAN

"Crane." Traditional Okinawan design in white on indigo fabric. Collection of Junco Pollack.

## Crane, Butterfly and Peony, and Midnight Star
Designs for embroidery or quilting

The enduring quality of Japanese folk art is its ability to fulfill its function, without insistence on individuality, mood, or caprice. Fine craftsmanship has a mysterious beauty of its own when it is complemented by genuine simplicity. The Japanese folk artist is not an amateur; he is a skilled professional developing from the long experience of a continuous tradition. Alternating rows of butterflies and peonies in a brick repeat against a lattice background is a flexible fabric design. The lattice design can be used alone or in conjunction with other symbols. A monogram can be substituted for the single crane in the lattice pattern. Portions of these designs can be used for decorative banding, pillows, or fabric yardage. They are ideal quilting patterns. A simple running stitch, with stitches and spacing all of the same size, done in pure bleached white six-strand embroidery floss or single-strand cotton matte needlepoint thread on dark indigo blue linen or sailcloth, is most effective. These designs can also be quilted by hand or machine-stitched.

Pillow covered with fabric in a traditional peony and butterfly design. Collection of Ron Ho.

58

*"Midnight Star." White running stitch on a dark background. Simple but effective, the design is easily duplicated with the aid of tracing paper and a ruler.*

**Crane**

17¾″ × 10¼″

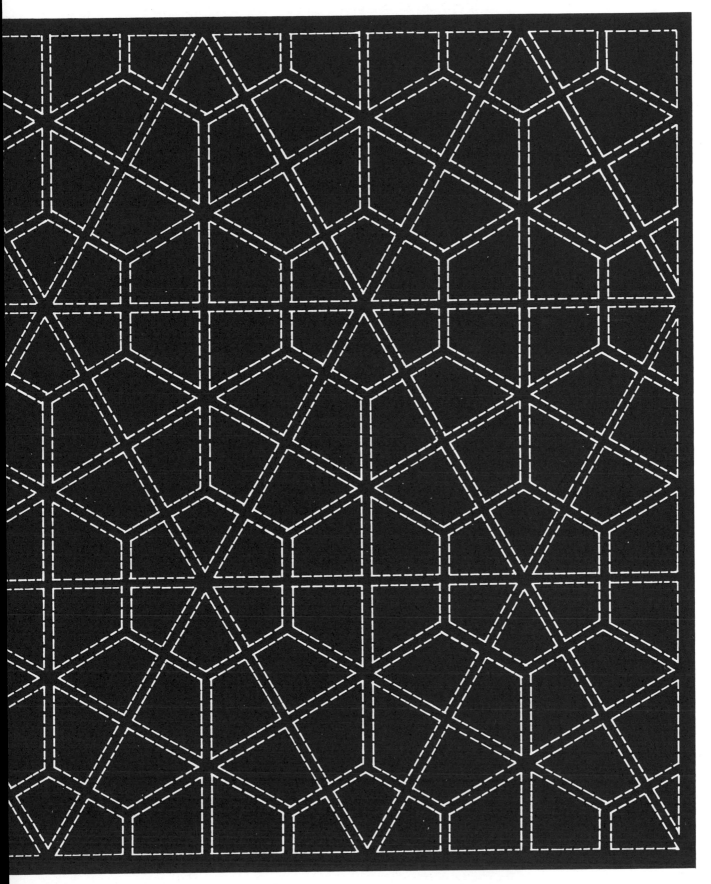

**Butterfly and Peony**

20″ × 15″

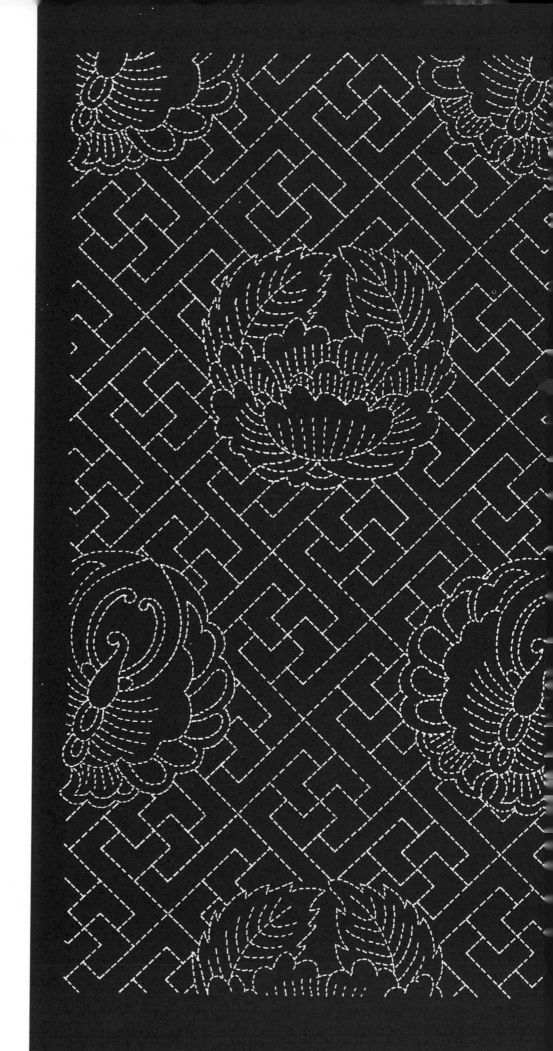

# List of Plates

1 Chimera.
2 Boy Riding Ch'i-lin.
3 Children at Play.
4 Immortality. *Executed by Belle Kicinski.*
5 Love.
6 Persian Pillow.
7 Memory of Isfahan. *Executed by Eleanor Bello Jani.*
8 Blue Tile.
9 Potpourri.
10 Persian Crest. *Designed and executed by Dolores Wiemann.*
11 Topkapi I. *Executed by Jan Silberstein.*
12 Topkapi II. *Executed by Diane Piemonte.*
13 Suleiman's Tughra. *Executed by Dolores Wiemann.*
14 Carnations.
15 Tantric Design for a Pillow.
16 Lotus Blossoms.
17 Star of India. *Executed by Susan Kicinski.*
18 Piggy Bank. *Executed by Dolores Wiemann.*
19 Garuda.
20 Arabesque. *Executed by Benine Adolf.*
21 Khan el Khalili.
22 Mamluk Border.

1

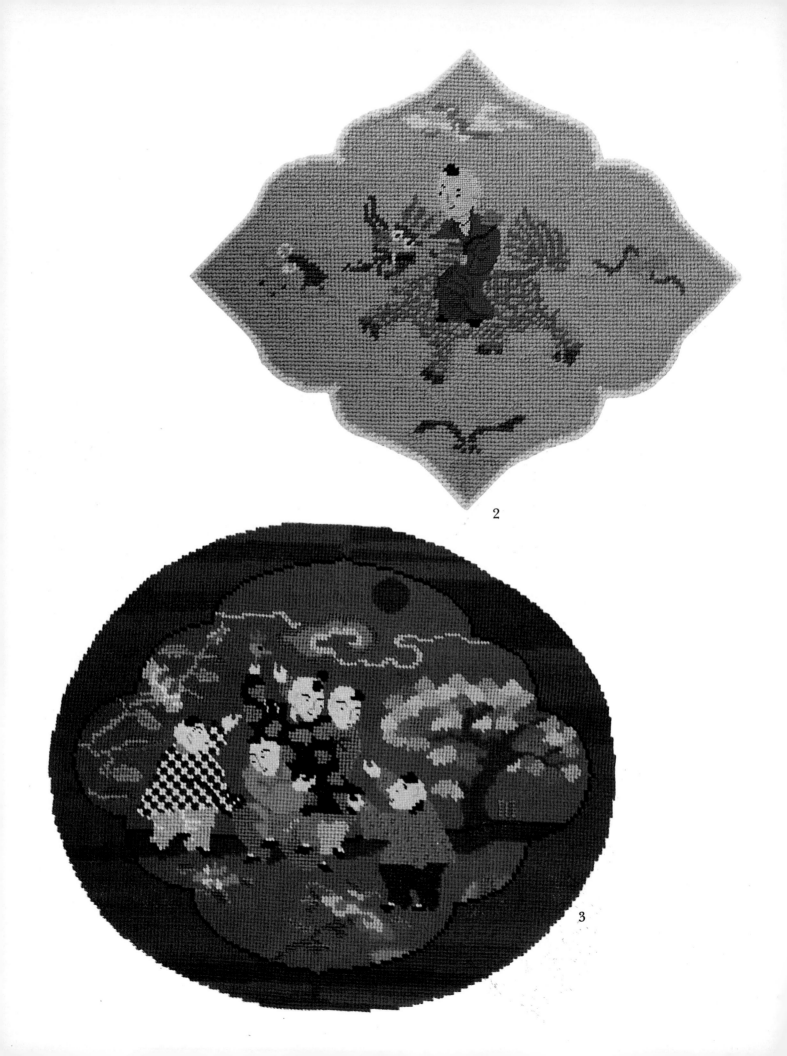

4

5

6

7

8

9

10

11

12

13

15

16

17

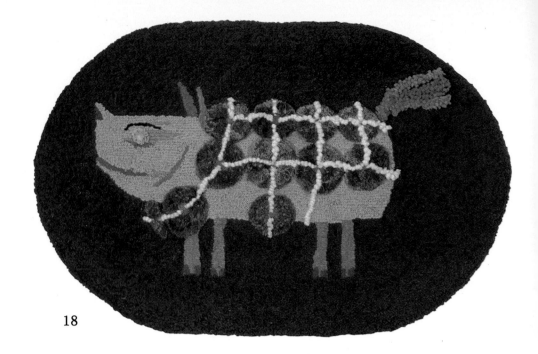

18

19

20

21

22

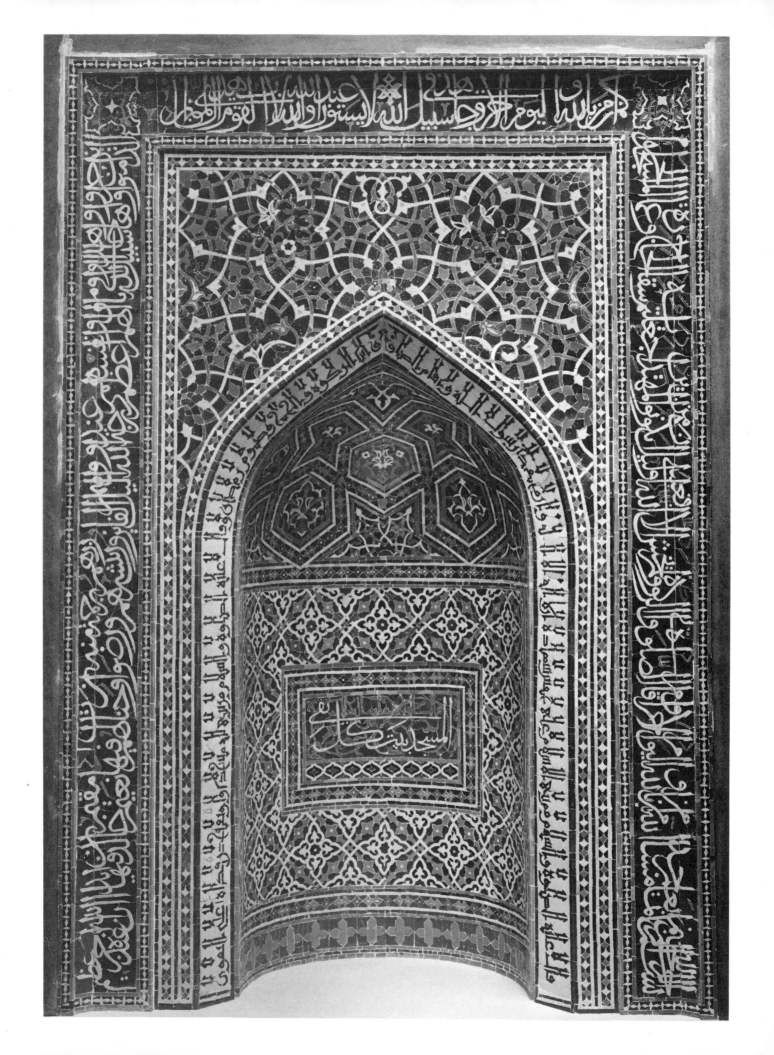

# Iran

Persian craftsmen have always been in great demand outside their own country, accounting, in part, for the diffusion of Persian art and culture to other groups as far to the west of Iran as Baghdad and Damascus, and to Samarkand in the east. Last of the native Persian rulers before the Islamic era, the Sasanians produced the earliest known textile examples in silk fabric, indicating a flourishing trade route to China or the possession of China's most cherished secret: sericulture. Firm contact with Chinese culture was established during the reign of Timur, or Tamerlane, a warrior from Central Asia of Turkic and Mongolian descent. Tamerlane solidified his wide conquests: he and his successors, the Timurids, ruled throughout the fourteenth and fifteenth centuries, encouraging Persian art and design through patronage.

The peony and the lotus so frequently described in Chinese art, as well as the Chinese cloud band, the dragon, and the phoenix, mingled with other Persian design elements. During this period experiments with lusters, porcelains, and glazes brought to new heights pottery beautifully decorated in turquoise green and dark blue. Brilliantly bold architectural tile work in turquoise blue banded with black was offset by the subtle, muted colors of a new art form: miniature paintings illustrating manuscripts. Persian miniatures illuminate the history of the times and reflect the decorative arts of the period.

The sixteenth and seventeenth centuries, marking a return to native rule under the Safavids, may very well have been the most creative in the history of Persian art. The flower, a predominant symbol of earthly beauty and peace for the Muslim, represented the possibility of even greater pleasures in another world. Early carpets were simple floral repeat units, but the glory of the Safavid court workshops was the central medallion set in a field of flowers, palmettes, and arabesques surrounded by formal floral borders. Many textiles were executed from designs created by court manuscript painters. Lavishly rich and beautiful colors were a tribute to the advancement of the dyer's art. Sumptuous silk, silver and gold metallic threads were used in textiles as well as carpets. Tabriz, Kashan, Herat, Isfahan, and Kirman are among the best known of the weaving centers.

*Iranian mihrab, or prayer niche, of glazed earthenware tiles set in plaster from the Madrasah Imami in Isfahan, built A.D. 1354. The Metropolitan Museum of Art, Harris Brisbane Dick Fund, 1939.*

*Border design derived from prayer niche mosaic.*

83

# Persian Pillow

(Plate 6)
Needlepoint
11½″ × 13¼″ (11¼″ × 13″ finished)
153 square inches

All of the elements in this design are to be found on the Iranian mihrab from the Madrasah Imami. The central leaf appearing in the foliate design just above the niche may have been derived from the delicate Japanese maple leaf, but more likely it represents a marijuana leaf. The colors used in the worked examples are:

Venetian red 211, 3 strands
Beige 593, 1 oz.
Turquoise 738, 1¼ oz.
Navy blue 742, ½ oz.
Light olive green 545, 1½ oz.

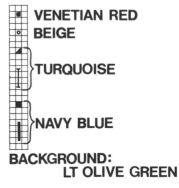

VENETIAN RED
BEIGE
TURQUOISE
NAVY BLUE
BACKGROUND:
    LT OLIVE GREEN

petit point

85

# Memory of Isfahan

(Plate 7)
Needlepoint
12¼″ × 13¼″
163 square inches

Exotic flowers call for unusual color schemes. Creative color schemes seem strangely different until they become familiar. This striking arrangement of brilliant Persian colors set against a background inspired by the desert sands was started with a double outline of medium blue and a warm golden brown. Rice stitch adds dimensionality to the pollen area of the flower. The petal in purple bargello has enough visual weight to stand out against the weighty seeds. Experiment with color for filling the petal areas. Set the picture plane deeper with contrasting borders of cashmere stitch. The colors in the example shown in Plate 7 are:

Light turquoise 738, ½ oz.
Dark turquoise 773, ½ oz.
Medium blue 741, ½ oz.
Dark blue 723, ¼ oz.
Red R50, ¼ oz.
Vivid pink 829, 8 strands
Magenta 644, 1 oz.
Purple 642, 5 strands
Medium golden brown 411, ½ oz.
Golden tan 466, 1 oz.

# Blue Tile

(Plate 8)
Needlepoint, petit point, or cross-stitch embroidery
3″ repeat border on 10-mesh canvas or Aida cloth or 2¼″ border
   on 16-mesh canvas

An infinite variety of design motifs can be derived from the mosaic tiles used on a single prayer niche. Organic colors ground from semiprecious stones or dug from the earth's clay deposits blend harmoniously with their environment. Glazed earthenware tiles are richly colored with the natural blues of lapis lazuli and cobalt, offset with charcoal black, white, and the warm spice color of sienna.

This faience tile pattern might be used to make a belt, a border, an eyeglass case, or an all-over pattern. Repeat units can be halved to fit specific lengths. Small repeat borders in contrasting colors might be added to extend the width. Eyeglasses should fit snugly in their case with no chance of sliding out

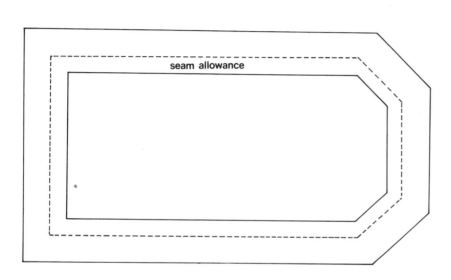

seam allowance

*Diagram for cutting canvas for an eyeglass case. To make a pattern, measure an old case in a size appropriate to the glasses. In the design area, allow for depth as well as length and width. Cut two pieces. In addition to the seam allowance, the pattern includes ⅝″ of extra canvas all around to be taped to prevent fraying as you work. When the needlepoint is finished, stitch back and front together along the inner solid line, trimming off the excess at the dotted cutting line.*

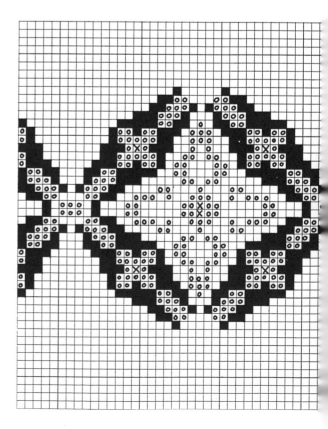

*Hexagonal design using motifs from the mihrab.*

when the case is turned upside down. Check the pattern size against an old case and sew a felt lining together as a guide in determining the size of the needlepoint outer case. A belt done in needlepoint on canvas can be finished with a suede or felt lining. A belt worked in cross-stitch on Aida cloth may require a backing of Pellon or other stiffening material.

Colors used in the example shown in Plate 8 are:

Royal blue 723
Medium light blue 754
Sienna red 211
White 005

*Eyeglass case in "Blue Tile" design.*

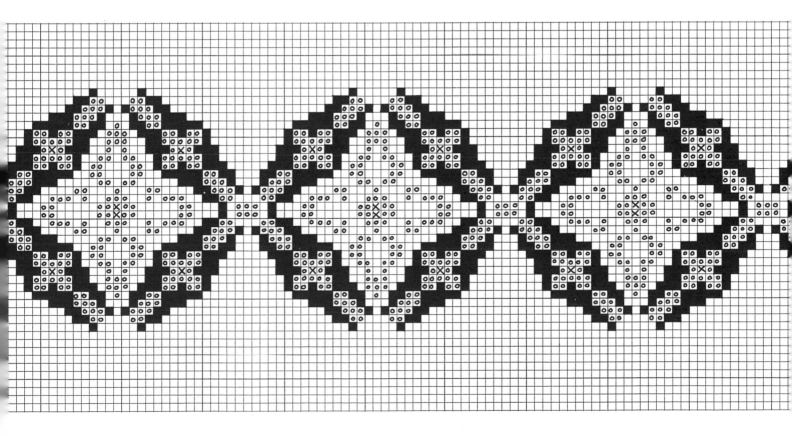

## Ibex

Free Machine Stitchery

The glory of Persian art flourished centuries before the Islamic period. A sensitive Achaemenian sculptor lovingly modeled and cast in bronze a sophisticated and realistic yet stylized ibex. The strong simplicity of its forms makes it an excellent subject for interpretation in free stitchery.

*Bronze head of an ibex. Achaemenian period, fifth to fourth century B.C. The Metropolitan Museum of Art, Fletcher Fund, 1956.*

# Potpourri

(Plate 9)
Crewel embroidery

Potpourri is a medley of flowers and arabesques designed for the encrustation of fabric with jewel-colored wools. Solidly cover an even-weave fabric with couching and satin stitch. Use every bit of excess wool left from other projects. Choose a soft open weave fabric such as monk's cloth, Duraback, or a sturdy wool fabric with a fifty-fifty weave for easy stitching with two- or three-ply Persian yarn. Heavier yarns, or yarns doubled over, should be couched to the surface with matching or contrasting single-ply yarn.

# Persian Crest

(Plate 10)
Hooked rug
19″ × 4′ 6″

A small detail selected from an intricate Oriental rug provided the inspiration for this design for a hooked runner. Previously unseen images of the heads of birds arranged in series became obvious upon enlargement of the detail. In the example shown in Plate 10, multiple outlines in black, red, and pink add depth to a design having no depth. Speckling on the birds was achieved by using wool fabrics with pronounced tweed or checkered patterns. Many shades of blue, blue-green, and tan are highlighted with touches of bright pink against a wine-red background.

The crest has been duplicated at either end of the runner. For a central medallion on a rug place units in the north, east, south, and west positions and almost touching each other.

Advancing eastward through southern Russia and Iran, nomadic Turkish tribes from Central Asia who had been converts to Islam in the ninth century soon began to erode the Byzantine Empire. The Ottoman Turks expanded their power through frequent wars against the Balkan states, and in 1453 captured Constantinople, the last stronghold of the Eastern Roman Empire with its vast accumulation of the ancient arts.

Under the reign of Suleiman the Magnificent, the sixteenth century was the finest period in the decorative arts of the Muslim world. Tradition has it that the first "Persian" carpets to be imported into Europe came from Turkey rather than Persia; more likely they actually were made in Egypt. The so-called Holbein carpets shown in Dutch and Italian paintings are a mixture of the Egyptian Mamluk and the Turkish Ottoman styles. Early silk prayer rugs with a center motif of a mihrab, or prayer niche, patterned after those in the walls of mosques, were woven from designs prepared by Ottoman court artists and produced in both Egyptian and Turkish court factories. Ushak, Ghiordes, Lâdik, Kula, and Bergama are familiar names of towns noted for the production of Turkish carpets.

The opulence of the Sultan and his courtiers was unsurpassed. Istanbul's Topkapi Museum is a treasury for the staggering wealth of Suleiman, containing, in addition to his solidly encrusted diamond throne, luxurious caftans, banners, cushions, and fabrics shimmering with gold and silver threads. Tulips and carnations were favored in the garden as well as on fabrics that were produced in a limited color scheme of rich reds, blues, and greens. Flowers were loved for themselves without ritualistic meaning. Stylized rather than naturalistic in accord with Muslim rejection of idolatry, the floral forms complemented Islamic symbols.

*Late-sixteenth-century mosque lamp. The Metropolitan Museum of Art.*

*Turkish sixteenth-century wall tile in two tones of blue on white. The Metropolitan Museum of Art, gift of Horace Havemeyer, 1940.*

*Design for embroidery taken from the
bowl of the dish opposite.*

*Glazed faience dish from Asia Minor.
Late sixteenth century. The Metro-
politan Museum of Art, bequest of
Isaac D. Fletcher, 1917.*

*Double panel of velvet brocade in crimson and gold. Turkish, sixteenth century. The Metropolitan Museum of Art, Rogers Fund, 1917.*

# Topkapi

(Plates 11 and 12)
Needlepoint
14″ × 15″ (finished size 13¾″ × 14¾″)
210 square inches

This adaptation of a celebrated six-teenth-century Turkish cut-velvet brocade in crimson and gold is presented in two versions in Plates 11 and 12. One color scheme was selected by closely matching the colors in an Oriental car-pet, the other with royal burgundy, sil-ver, and gold, a personal conception of unusually luxurious color. If you were asked to choose an opulent color scheme, what would your choice be?

In Plate 11 the center seed pod is outlined with Elsa Williams Cloisonné gold polyester needlepoint thread and filled with gold and silver thread in addition to many shades of DMC cotton floss, including pink, peach, burnt orange, and old rose, and is surrounded by burnt-orange velvet chenille. Suc-ceeding forms are filled with pink and peach six-strand cotton floss, royal bur-gundy Persian yarns, burnt-orange vel-vet chenille, and salmon and orange cotton floss on a royal burgundy back-ground. The DMC cotton floss was used doubled on the 10-mesh canvas.

The colors used in the example in Plate 12 are:

Dark Venetian red 210, 1½ oz.
Medium Venetian red 215, 8 strands
Medium blue-grey 314, ¾ oz.
Medium green 522, ¼ oz.
Dark mustard 521, 1 oz.
Medium yellow-green 553, 6 strands
Pale green 563, ¼ oz.
Dark olive green 540, ½ oz.
Gold 445, ½ oz.
Light tan 138, ½ oz.
Red R50, 2 strands
Light orange 444, 4 strands

# Suleiman's Tughra

(Plate 13)
Hooked rug
20″ × 30″

*Tughra of Suleiman the Magnificent from an imperial edict. Gouache and gold leaf on paper. The Metropolitan Museum of Art, Rogers Fund, 1938.*

The official signature of Suleiman the Magnificent, ruling Sultan of Turkey from 1520 to 1566, is an elaborate calligraphic symbol called a tughra. It is considered one of the most original creations in Ottoman art—there is no comparable form in the Muslim world. Its fluid lines have a lyrical quality and allow easy arrangements in a variety of sequences to fit different proportions. One, two, or more of the single units can be joined to form entirely new designs. Expand the central space for a longer surface or lengthen the straight exterior lines to fit irregular shapes. The hearth rug was hand-hooked with a small crochet hook by pulling narrowly cut strips of wool fabric from the under surface through a monk's cloth backing to the top surface in a short loop. This design is also suitable for gros point, using a 5-mesh canvas and rug yarn.

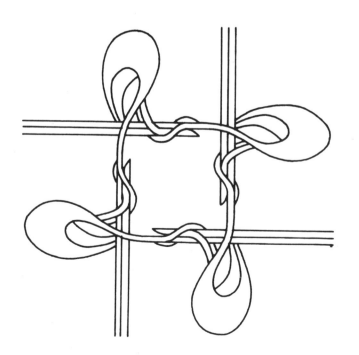

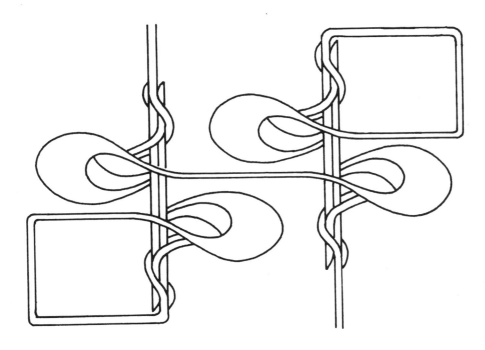

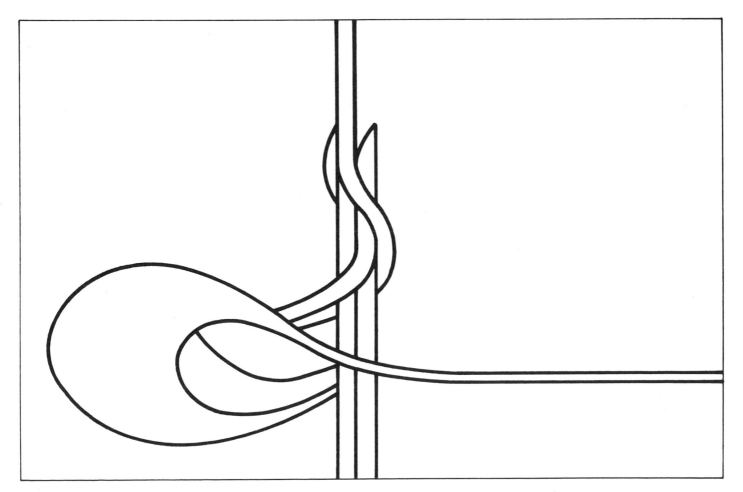

104

# Syria

Syria, situated on the trade and military routes between the East and the West, was the crossroads for the spread of Islamic art through North Africa and Southern Europe. It is said Paul was converted to Christianity on the road to Damascus, Syria's capital city. All roads led to Damascus, and a history of one conquest after another resulted in cultural mixture and political laxity until the appearance, in the seventh century A.D., of the Arabs, when the region became integrated under Islamic rule. With the introduction of the Islamic genius for absorbing the creative aspects of other cultures, all the arts flourished. The legacy of the lavish Byzantine culture that had existed in Syria before the arrival of the Omayyad Caliphs set the tone for the building of elaborate mosques opulently constructed of Syrian limestone and Lebanese cedar and decorated with the material resources of Islam's vast empire.

Damascus was noted for silks and woolens, furniture inlaid with mother-of-pearl and mosaic forms of marquetry, and for metalwork, luster glass, and ceramics. Damask (named for Damascus) is a rich reversible fabric with a variety of complex patterns formed in the weaving. Exquisite Islamic designs in silk and satin were sometimes woven with the addition of gold and silver threads. Damascus was also world-renowned for the beauty of its swords and other arms; indeed, the term damascening, which refers to a technique of inlaying decorations of gold and silver on iron, steel, brass, or bronze, derives from the city's name. In addition, various kinds of vessels, including those with glaze enameling on glass (called porcelainized glass) were the result of the Damascenes' technical finesse. Mosque lamps and glass objects for the royal table were delicately gilded with pen and brush to form designs and were kiln-fired. The design outlines were then delineated in red and thickly covered with enameling glaze color before being fired again for a final fusing. These Syrian glass lamps, sometimes filled partway with water on which oil and a wick were floated, were decorated with dedications and inscriptions from the Koran, enhanced by bands of rosettes and stylized flowers.

*Syrian pottery tile from the end of the sixteenth century. The Metropolitan Museum of Art, bequest of Edward C. Moore, 1891.*

# Carnations

(Plate 14)
Crewel embroidery
10″½ × 12″

Although this design is derived from a Syrian tile, it is also typical of Persian and Turkish Islamic art. The two-thousand-year-old pink, also called a carnation because of its flesh color, is the basis for almost two thousand other varieties, both single- and double-petaled, in assorted roseate colors. In this design some of the carnations are embroidered in blue for cool contrast. The finished example shown in color was made on cotton twill with single strands of three-ply Persian yarn in the following shades:

**Violet flowers**
Medium violet 618
Dark medium violet 615
Dark violet 642
Rose 228
Wine 295
Magenta 644

**Blue flowers**
Light blue 743
Medium blue 741
Dark medium blue 733
Dark blue 742

**Pink flowers**
Vivid shocking pink Columbia
    Minerva 847c

**Coral flowers**
Coral 255
Pink 831
Dark red 231

**Leaves and stems**
Light green G74
Medium light green 574
Medium green G64
Dark green G54

**Vase**
White 011
Medium blue 741
Dark blue 742
Deep purple 610

**Tile base**
Light turquoise 748
Medium turquoise 728
Dark turquoise 718
Gold 427

106

*Designs of tulips and carnations adapted from Syrian ceramic tile.*

*Left: Ceramic tile from the beginning of the seventeenth century. The Metropolitan Museum of Art, Rogers Fund, 1907.*

108

109

# India

Isolated for thousands of years by the Himalayan mountain ranges of Tibet and Afghanistan and by the sea, India developed an unusually personal culture with unique customs. Many Indian philosophies and their visual and ceremonial symbols are appealing to Westerners. Yoga, for instance, is a popular Tantric ritual for developing concentration so that one may become aware of all that is dormant in the unconscious. Tantra art forms, derived from the geometric cosmology of the astronomy-minded Jain sect, are universally known. These triangular arrangements in sharp, bright colors are used alone or in combination with other symbols, usually the lovely petaled lotus.

The diversity of Indian peoples from antiquity to the present is evident in the complex religions and the many different languages. Although most of the early Hindu and Jain monuments have disappeared, there remain hundreds of stunning architectural examples, built of permanent materials, representing Buddhist and Mughal influence, in addition to those of the later Hindu and Jain periods. Bell-shaped, ornately carved temples, massive forts, domed mausoleums, and luxurious palaces are often covered with sculpture illustrating Indian life, its religious aspects and preoccupations. Figurative sculpture is voluptuous, clearly erotic, vital and energetic during the Buddhist period and somewhat stiff and expressionless in form during the Jain period. Even the incursion of the Romans is reflected in the classically robed and coiffed Gandharan style.

The cottage industries of India have supported incredibly skilled craftsmen. Since ancient times Indian artisans have produced superb textiles, brocaded, embroidered, painted, dyed, and elaborately woven with gold thread. During the ascendency of the Mughals (descendants of Tamerlane), the technique of carpet weaving was introduced, probably by Persian craftsmen. Islamic floral designs were used in a less complex manner.

Precisely illustrated manuscripts, delicately detailed and colored, are closely related to Persian miniature paintings and are sometimes mistaken for them, partly because Hindu classics were often translated into Persian, the Mughal court language.

*Silk thread embroidery in a detail of cotton bedspread from southern India, c. 1700. Museum of Fine Arts, Boston, gift of Mrs. Frank M. Clark.*

*Traditional representation of Indian epic figure carved in wood. Author's collection.*

111

# Tantric Design for a Pillow

(Plate 15)
Needlepoint
12⅝″ × 12⅝″
159 square inches

This design was inspired by the symbolism found in eighteenth-century Rajasthan Tantra painting. According to Ajit Mookerjee in *Tantra Art: Its Philosophy and Physics*, the encompassing circle represents ignorance, the eight lotus petals are earth, heaven, water, fire, air, the mind, the intellect, and egoism, and the series of triangles indicate knowledge and the senses. The example in Plate 15 was worked in the following shades:

Red R10, 24 yards
Orange 960, 13 yards
Lemon yellow 450, 37 yards
Dark pink 649, 20 yards
Medium pink 828, 8 yards
Light pink 256, 12 yards
Pale pink 831, 6 yards
White 011, 73 yards

RED
ORANGE
LEMON YELLOW
DK PINK
MED PINK
LT PINK
PALE PINK
BACKGROUND: WHITE

petit point

# Lotus Blossoms

(Plate 16)
Embroidery

This lotus blossom in its traditional Tantric position may be used as a single unit or an endless vertical running border. The design can be enlarged or reduced to fit specific projects. A combination of split, satin, and stem stitch is used. Consider a combination of appliqué and embroidery. The color example was embroidered on silk shantung with three strands of six-strand cotton floss and with number 8 cotton perle thread in the following DMC shades:

Pale pink 225
Pink 3689
Dark pink 605
Rose 603
Dark rose 602
Red 321
Gold 742
Orange 947
Dark blue-grey 930

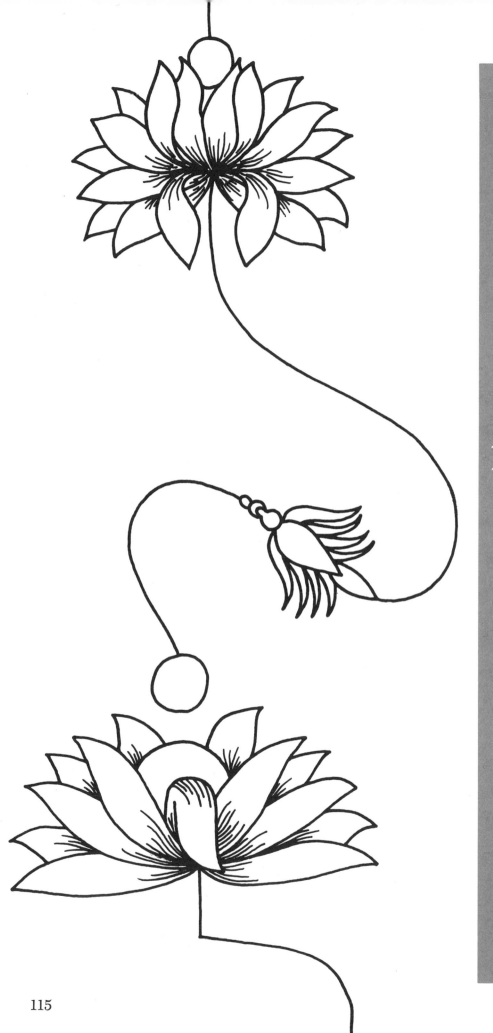

# Star of India

(Plate 17)
Patchwork coverlet

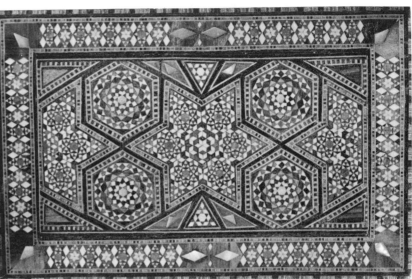

*Marquetry box lid. The central motif inspired the "Star of India" patchwork design.*

Marquetry, a piecing together of veneers of rare colored woods and precious materials such as ivory and mother-of-pearl, perfectly fitted like patchwork, is fast becoming a lost art. This five-foot mosaic of patchwork radiating from a central star reproduces the colors of the natural woods and ivory of a finely crafted marquetry jewel box. In the finished patchwork the star is padded and appliquéd to the background fabric of the coverlet.

*The complete star.*

116

*Measurement for the border sections
of "Star of India."*

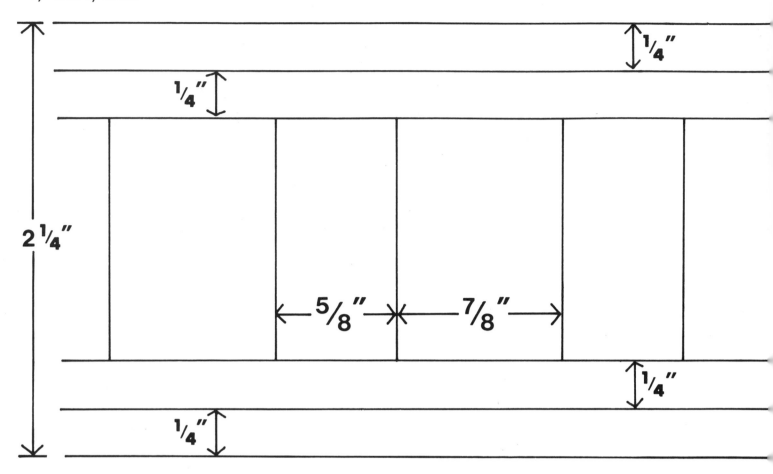

$2\frac{1}{4}''$

$\frac{1}{4}''$

$\frac{1}{4}''$

$\frac{1}{4}''$

$\frac{1}{4}''$

$\frac{5}{8}''$

$\frac{7}{8}''$

1

*Templates for the patchwork pieces
include seam allowances.*

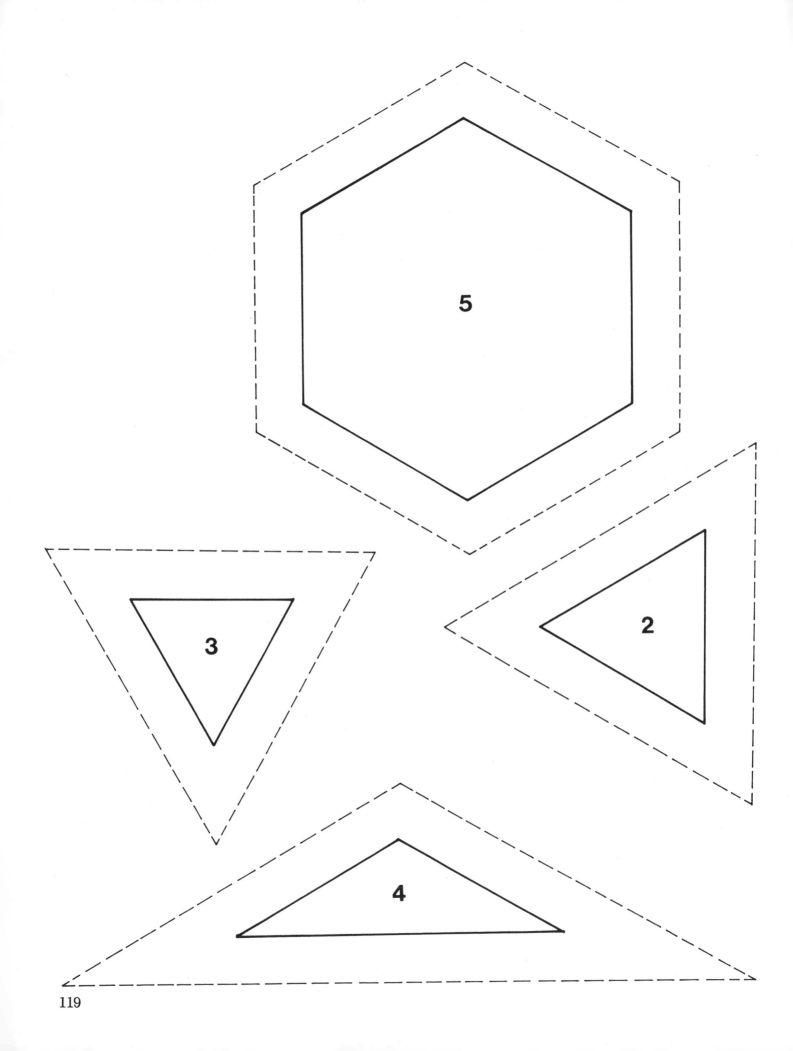

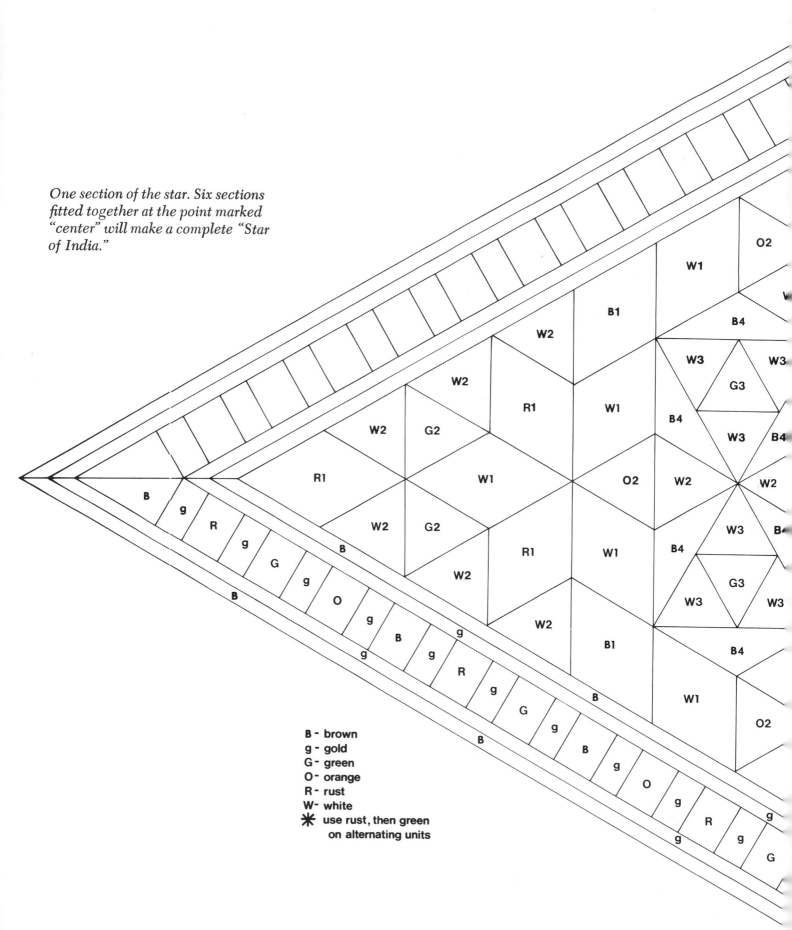

*One section of the star. Six sections fitted together at the point marked "center" will make a complete "Star of India."*

B - brown
g - gold
G - green
O - orange
R - rust
W - white
✱ use rust, then green on alternating units

120

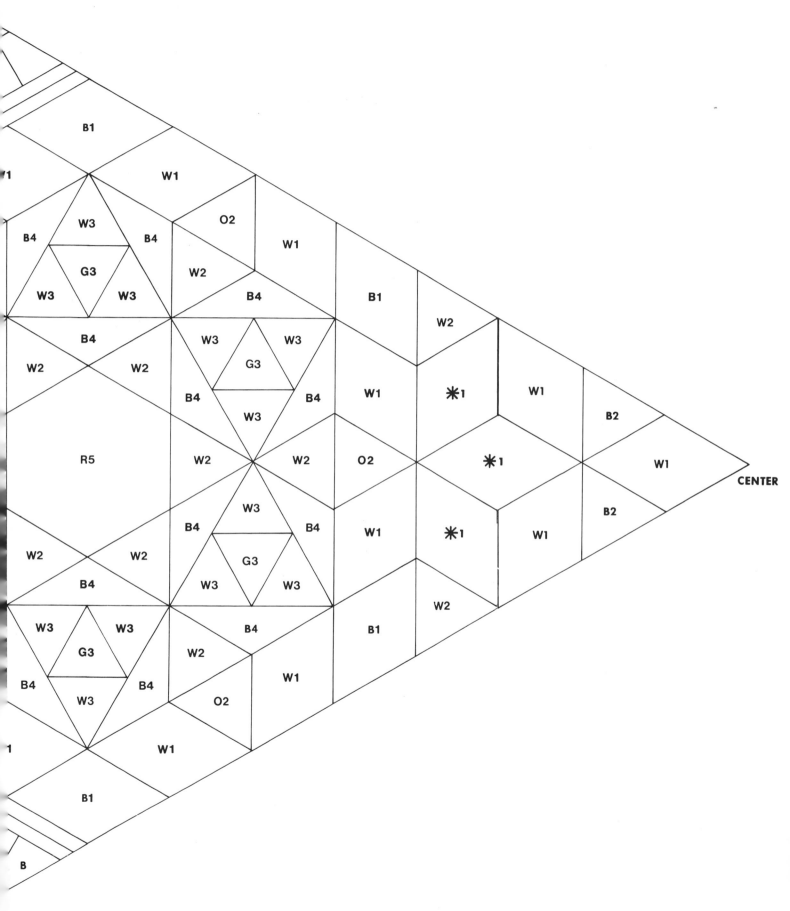

CENTER

# Indonesia

Indian influence prevailed in the arts and architecture of Indonesia, mainly in Java, Sumatra, and Bali. The finest Indonesian monument is in Java; Borobudur contains innumerable niches from which images of Buddha formerly faced outward. It is a mountain temple of stone, placed at what was considered the metaphysical center of the world. Enormous circular terraces are topped with seventy-two additional open latticework, bell-shaped stupas, or domes, which held images of Buddha. Sculptured reliefs illustrated a series of religious themes. During the sixteenth century the arrival of the Muslims forced the Hindu rajahs of Java to move their courts and ceremonial forms to Bali, where the indigenous culture diluted the spirit of the religious art. Temples built at a later date were decorated with sculpture in flatter relief, which suggests Balinese *wayang* puppets with their profile heads and feet, frontal bodies, and raiment of floral patterns representative of local batik textiles.

Today masked dancers re-enact the legends in the courtyards of Bali's many ancient and decaying temples, but tourists have given the spectacle a commercial aspect. In addition, mass production of shoddy hand-painted and batik textiles, masks, puppets, and other simple folk crafts has compounded the deterioration of the native arts.

On warm tropical islands where barter is a way of life, the imposition of other cultures can result in some unusual interpretations. The delightful pig laced with Chinese coins, a coinage in use on Bali years ago, may once have been representative of a family's wealth. It presents an amusing suggestion for a modern piggy bank.

*Indonesian masks of carved wood.*

123

# Piggy Bank

(Plate 18)
Design for hooking

*Black and gold wooden pig from Bali. The coins are Chinese. Author's collection.*

"Piggy Bank" is a suitable design for a small child's room. The subject matter can be arranged to fit a chair seat or to make an area rug, a pillow, or a picture. The design might be adapted for needlepoint or gros point. It is broad enough in its possibilities of interpretation to be used for appliquéing decorative accessories. The example in Plate 18 is a hooked seat cushion for a toy box.

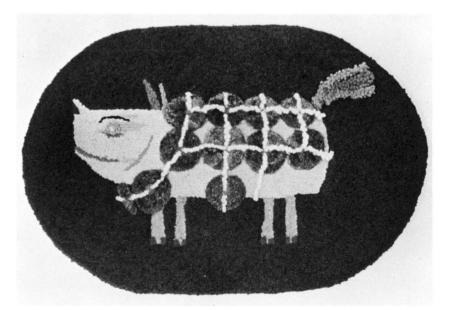

# Thailand

An acceptance of Indian forms and ideas is apparent in decorative art and architecture throughout Southeast Asia. It has often been said in the West that art is a reflection of the times, but because the basic premise governing Indian philosophies is the relationship of everything human to the divine, art is a phenomenon inseparable from life. Art forms are sacred, universal, and ritualistic, accounting for the similarity in design everywhere Buddhist thought is pervasive. Within that structure there are differences, personal adaptations and interpretations. Sculpture is the major art of the Thais, especially that cast in bronze, although other materials, such as stone and cement, are also used. The belief that the power of a sacred Buddha, which the Thais also interpreted as magical and supernatural, could be absorbed through precise duplication has resulted in the mass production of scores of barely distinguishable imitations and reproductions manufactured during every century. Some of the shrines have hundreds of statues of Buddha placed in endless rows.

Inordinately gilded nineteenth-century Thai temples, their gables and eaves rising sinuously in flamelike forms to pointed tips, seem more in keeping with theatrical designs for *Anna and the King of Siam* than their sacred prototypes. Burmese invasions account for the flamboyant points on Buddha heads and building tips and for the gilded glory of the guardian figures of birds and animals; later European influences imposed an order expressed in the formality of the topiary gardens and added an aura of comic opera to the statuary.

Among the minor arts popular throughout Southeast Asia is the shadow theater. Shadow plays performed with lacy silhouette figures intricately cut out of parchment began in China and became very popular all across India before spreading into Thailand and Cambodia. Drama, music, and dance are effective means of keeping legends alive.

*Asian shadow puppet.*

*Metal box from Thailand in the form of a mythical beast. Collection of Ramona Solberg.*

127

# Celestial Musician

Blackwork stitchery

Common figures in Southeast Asian art are *gandharvas*, celestial musicians who entertain gods and heroes in heaven. Undoubtedly, these gracefully voluptuous young women appeared bare-breasted at their performances, but carried away by the intricacies of calculating blackwork stitches, our prudish needle went too far. Draw your tracing carefully, making a minimum of lines to maintain a clean, clear working surface. Check the areas to be filled; ripping mars the fabric.

*"Celestial Musician" completed in blackwork stitchery.*

*Blackwork stitches for "Celestial Musician."*

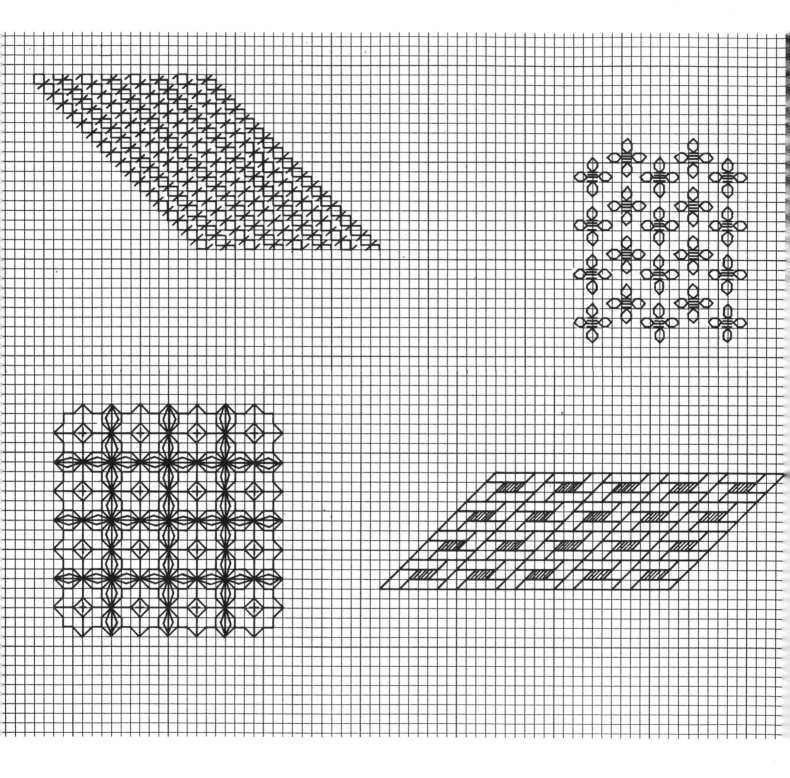

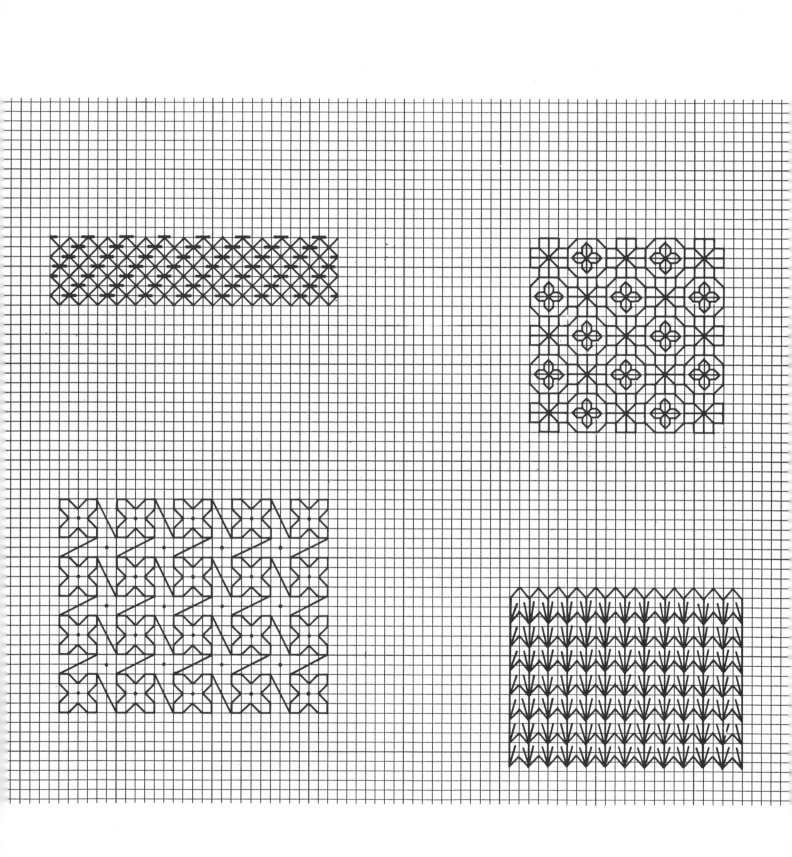

# Cambodia

Absolute perfection in Southeastern Asian art can be found hidden within a clearing of a few square miles in the Cambodian jungle. Neither words nor photographs can communicate the awesome grey stone beauty of Angkor Wat and Angkor Thom. Walled and surrounded by a moat like a fairy castle, Angkor Thom, the Khmer (Cambodian) capital, flourished from the ninth into the thirteenth century, only to be reclaimed by the encroaching jungle in the fifteenth century. Broad causeways crossing the moat are guarded by immense stone towers carved with calm, serene, enigmatically smiling faces welcoming visitors from all directions. Avenues leading to the buildings are lined with double rows of great seated figures holding tremendously long cobras. Full-scale processionals of elephants in bas relief line other avenues. Tigers, elephants, water buffalo, and snakes are native to the semitropical jungles of Cambodia. Temple guardians today are saffron-robed Buddhist monks who go silently about their chores amid grazing water buffalo and stately peacocks.

Angkor Wat is a separate temple complex, south of the city and reached by a six-hundred-foot causeway. Bell-shaped towers, bubbling with carving, rise above a temple on a stepped plateau built to resemble mountains, a site from which Hindu priests and kings could contact the divinities. The five-towered stone temple mountain of Angkor Wat has a two-hundred-foot central dome reached by a perilously steep flight of high, upright steps leading to a shrine dedicated to Vishnu. Galleries surrounding and leading to the shrine contain miles of figurative bas reliefs depicting episodes from Hindu legends, and also include representations of the classically beautiful *apsarases*, celestial dancers who symbolize sensual pleasures awarded in heaven.

*Apsaras. Charcoal temple rubbing.*

*Charcoal temple rubbing, the model for the "Peacock and Princeling" design.*

**Peacock and Princeling**

Temple rubbing rendered as a design for machine stitchery, embroidery, or blackwork.

134

Design for blackwork or embroidery.

135

# Garuda

(Plate 19)
Needlepoint
15½″ × 17½″ (finished size 15¼″ × 17¼″)
272 square inches

Representations of the half-human, half-animal mythological figure Garuda are seen in temple sculpture throughout Southeast Asia. When he is depicted holding a sword, his function is to fight off evil spirits.

This design was taken from a charcoal temple rubbing. A wide range of grey values was used to maintain the quality of the original stone carving. The grey values are warm and cool. Pale blue-violet is a cool grey with a bluish cast, light grey-violet is a warm grey with a lavender-pink cast. After choosing a variety of warm and cool greys in graduated shades from a yarn chart, cut and tape short lengths to a card and mark each one with an appropriate symbol from the diagram for easy reference while stitching. The example in Plate 19 was done in three-ply Persian yarn in the following shades:

Charcoal black 304, ¼ oz.
Pale blue-violet 641, ½ oz.
Medium blue-violet 631, 2 strands
Warm brown 110, ¼ oz.
Dark grey-violet 117, ½ oz.
Medium grey-violet 127, ½ oz.
Light grey-violet 137, ½ oz.
Pale grey-violet 660, ½ oz.
Warm pearl white 147, 4 oz.

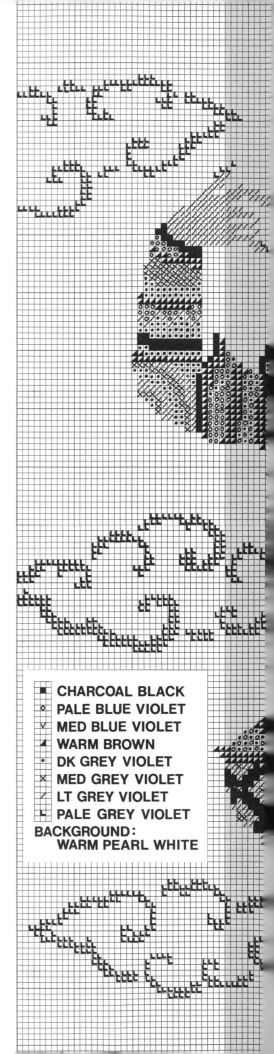

■ CHARCOAL BLACK
◦ PALE BLUE VIOLET
∨ MED BLUE VIOLET
◀ WARM BROWN
· DK GREY VIOLET
✕ MED GREY VIOLET
∠ LT GREY VIOLET
∟ PALE GREY VIOLET
BACKGROUND:
    WARM PEARL WHITE

*A detail of an Islamic mosque hang-
ing. Author's collection.*

# Egypt

One of the most spectacular civilizations of the ancient world developed in Egypt under the Pharaohs. With the occupation of Egypt by the Arabs between A.D. 639 and 642, stylistic conventions that had their beginnings in the fourth century B.C. and had survived Nubian, Assyrian, Persian, Greek, and Roman invasions underwent their most radical change. Along with a new language and a new religion, the Arabs brought new art forms to Egypt. In the tenth century A.D., rulers who claimed descent from Mohammed's daughter Fatimah established a new Islamic dynasty with Cairo as their capital. Imbued with the vigor of their Berber origins, the Fatimids inspired a superb period in the history of Egyptian architecture, ceramics, glassmaking, textiles, and metalwork. The beauty of Cairo resides in her mosques, with their tall, slender minarets. The oldest Fatimid architectural example (A.D. 970), the mosque and university of Al Azhar, remains unchanged today.

Fabrics produced at the state factories under the Fatimids were woven tapestries of linen richly embroidered with Kufic inscriptions. The tapestry technique was absorbed from the Copts, a Christian sect whose art had blossomed in Egypt in the fifth and sixth centuries, immediately before the Arab invasion. In embroideries the lion was a common symbol, as most luxury fabrics were used for the robes of state worn by kings and princes.

Geometric designs are the main feature of Islamic art. Infinite patterns were created by building outward from a pointed star shape, adding elongated triangular forms in a continuous repetition of geometric arrangements. Arabesques often fill the open compartments of the forms. The stalactite vault is an example of a three-dimensional ceiling sculpture formed of geometric patterns.

The uprising of slave against master gave rise to the Mamluk (the word means slave) dynasty in the fifteenth century, an era marked by further advancement in the decorative arts. Royal patronage of the factories ceased to exist, but production continued. A Mamluk carpet is distinguished by its unusual two-color scheme of deep ruby red and spring green. Sometimes the deep red is combined with a delicate blue-violet. The pattern is a complex of octagonal, lozenge-shaped, star, circular, and triangular medallions. Every inch of the background and interior space is filled with formalized foliate designs. The Mamluk dynasty disappeared with the sweep of the Ottoman Turks across North Africa and their occupation of Egypt in the sixteenth century, but the carpet factories survived.

# Arabesque

(Plate 20)
Needlepoint or appliqué
11" × 28½" (finished size 10½" × 28")
Approximately 314 square inches

"Arabesque" was adapted from an appliqué mosque hanging and can be stitched as needlepoint on canvas or as appliqué in cotton fabric or felt. The needlepoint diagram shows one half of the geometric Arabesque design, graphed to the center point. Reverse this symmetrical design by turning the diagram upside down and add the other half by fitting the "center" marks. Arabesque was designed as a pillow bolster for a studio couch. The size can easily be adjusted by increasing or decreasing the borders. Further decreases in size for a sofa pillow can be made by using 12- or 14-mesh canvas. Choose colors suitable to your interior. Those used in the example in Plate 20 are:

Dark green 557, 2 oz.
Royal blue 740, 1½ oz.
Black 050, 10 yards
Bright orange 968, 8 yards
Medium light aqua 738, ¾ oz.
Red 242, 1 oz.
White 011, 1½ oz.

*A rectangular detail of the mosque hanging.*

*"Arabesque" as appliqué.*

*"Arabesque" outlined for embroidery.*

center

center

*Detail of an appliquéd mosque hanging.*

145

# Khan el Khalili

(Plate 21)
Needlepoint
15″ × 15″ (finished size 14½″ × 14½″)
225 square inches

The distribution of colors has not been indicated on this diagram. Choose a color scheme to complement your interior. The diagram appears in outline. Forms can be outlined in a contrasting color and the areas filled simply, or each form can be completely filled, one color set flush against another without an outline. Our finished example features liberal use of the rich colors that make Islamic mosaics so vibrantly attractive. The shades are:

Navy blue 721, 2 oz.
Medium blue-green 755, ½ oz.
Medium turquoise 738, ½ oz.
Gold 427, ½ oz.
Red R10, 9 strands
Cream 438, 2 oz.

*"Khan el Khalili" makes use of typical design forms.*

147

# Mamluk Border

(Plate 22)
Cross-stitch or appliqué

Adapted from an appliquéd mosque hanging and stitched in the original colors of black, red, spring green, and blue-violet, the Mamluk border shown in Plate 22 was specifically designed as decoration for the bottom of a swirling peasant skirt and the neckline and sleeves of a blouse. Lavishly decorate a full wrist-length sleeve with two vertical rows of embroidery, reversing the diagram for the second row. This design can be worked on Hardanger cloth by crossing over two spaces. Counted-thread embroidery is suitable for any even-spaced fabric, such as batiste, Indian muslin, or linen. The finished example was done on Aida cloth.

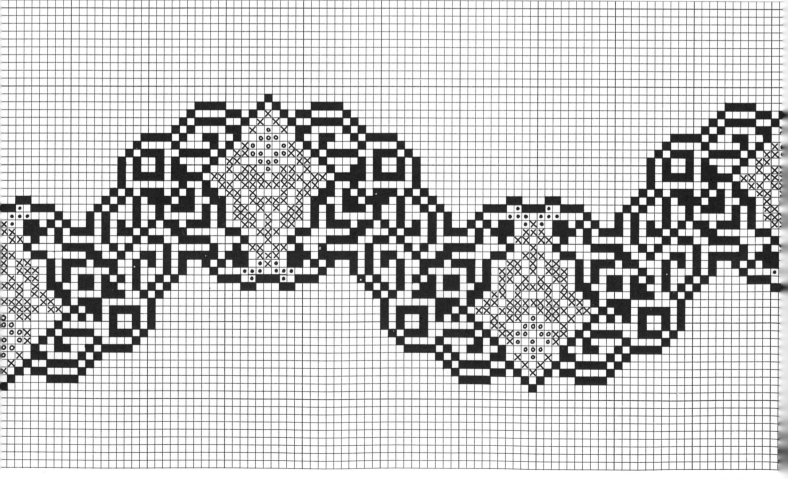

149

# Spain

When the Arabs crossed from North Africa to the Iberian peninsula, they brought with them the art and advanced technological achievements developed under many Islamic dynasties, indirectly benefiting the art of all Europe. Wherever the Muslims ruled they did not discard old forms to impose new ones; artistic conventions were absorbed or allowed to co-exist. In Spain the Omayyads, a branch of the Islamic dynasty which had its capital in Damascus, developed a brilliant civilization in Cordova. Decorative mosaic work on the Great Mosque there, elaborately ornamented with gold, was completed by Byzantine artists from Constantinople. There are records in the annals of the Vatican of silks produced in Spain during the ninth century, of silks used by the popes at Avignon or made into coronation robes for kings, and of the use of silks from floor to ceiling as adornment in the halls of the Alhambra.

To help contain the Christians, Muslims of Moroccan Berber stock were allowed to establish themselves in Spain. They made Seville their capital and created a new center of art and architecture there. The last Islamic dynasty in Spain was centered around the Alhambra in Granada, but was overthrown when the marriage of Isabella of Castile and Ferdinand of Aragon unified and strengthened Christian rule. Granada fell in 1492, permitting the Mudejars, those Muslims who wished to do so, to remain under Christian rule. Allowed to maintain their own way of life, they were highly productive during the thirteenth through fifteenth centuries. Silk textiles from Cordova, Seville, Almería, and Malaga dazzled both the Muslim and Christian worlds. Fabric designs with geometric patterns are generally attributed to Granada because of their similarity to the forms found in the many tile mosaics and elaborate stucco traceries on the ceilings, in the courtyards, and on the pillars of its buildings. A single such textile with interlocking motifs concerned with the idea of infinite pattern might have many totally different arrangements of design.

*Stars and diamonds dominate the pattern of this Alcazar mosaic.*

*Stalactite vault in the ceiling of the Alhambra.*

151

*Unusual among the Alhambra mosaics is this design which surrounds the characteristic star with curved forms.*

*Another Alhambra wall pattern.*

*Wall mosaic in the Alhambra in Granada. The pattern is executed in black, white, blue, green, turquoise, and yellow ochre tiles.*

# Alhambra

Quilted, appliquéd, or embroidered coverlet

*The complete "Alhambra" design.*

Muslim artists delighted in finding solutions to problems of geometric design, displaying the same intensity in their efforts as a devoted crossword puzzle fan. The walls of the Alhambra in Granada are covered with superb examples of geometric inlaid ceramic tile designs. Many of the patterns extend outward from a central star. Turquoise, royal blue, black, and white provide a cool, contemporary color scheme for a modern interior. This design for a coverlet consists of two distinct motifs repeated around a similar central theme. Each motif can be completed individually as stitchery or patchwork and appliquéd to a background fabric, or used separately as a design for a pillow cover. Trace and enlarge the line drawing on the opposite page to make a pattern for stitchery. Shaded drawings for making patterns for patchwork or appliqué are provided on pages 156 and 157.

For appliqué, put tracing paper over the shaded drawings and trace one example of each different piece in the design. Enlarge the drawings by the grid system or photostatically to the desired size. (For a double bed coverlet 78 inches wide, each drawing would have to be enlarged to approximately 6 times the size shown.) From the enlarged drawings, make cardboard or paper patterns for each piece, remembering to add a ¼-inch seam allowance to every one.

155

*The center medallion. Shaded areas show relative color values for appliqué or patchwork.*

*The side medallion and the square motif. Dark stippled areas are the background fabric of the coverlet.*

157

# List of Suppliers

Write to large wholesalers of yarn, fabric, and canvas for the names of retail department stores and stitchcraft shops in your vicinity carrying their products. Many wholesalers and retailers offer mail-order catalogues and swatch cards. When ordering by mail, color numbers, bits of yarn, or swatches of fabric are helpful in identifying specific colors. If large amounts of an individual color are needed, uncut hanks, generally weighing four ounces, are a saving when compared with individually cut strands.

## Wholesale suppliers

The DMC Corp., 107 Trumbull Street, Elizabeth, N.J. 07206. DMC embroidery cotton.

Paternayan Bros., Inc., 312 East 95th Street, New York, N.Y. 10028.

Columbia Minerva Corp., 295 Fifth Avenue, New York, N.Y. 10016.

Paragon Art and Linen Co., Inc., 367 Southern Boulevard, Bronx, N.Y. 10545.

Bucilla Co., 30–20 Thompson Avenue, Long Island City, N.Y. 11101. Bucilla yarns.

Appleton Bros. of London, West Main Road, Little Compton, R.I. 02857. Tapestry yarns.

## Mail-order houses

Lee Wards, P.O. Box 206, Elgin, Ill. 60120. General needlework supplies.

Belding Corticelli, Ltd., P.O. Box 9, Montreal 101, Quebec, Canada. DMC cotton.

## Mail order and retail

(*indicates catalogues available on request)

*Frederick J. Fawcett, Inc., 129 South Street, Boston, Mass. 02111. Linen yarns and threads.

The Yarn Depot, Inc., 545 Sutter Street, San Francisco, Calif. 94102. Unusual yarns.

In Stitches, 102 Yorkville Avenue, Toronto 5, Ontario, Canada.

Mary McGregor, P.O. Box 154, Englewood, Ohio 45322. Paternayan Persian and rug yarn.

*The Needlework Shop, Royal Ridge Mall, Nashua, N.H. 03060. Paternayan Persian yarns, DMC cotton, Aida and Hardanger cloths.

*Craft Yarns of Rhode Island, Inc., 603 Mineral Spring Avenue, Pawtucket, R.I. 02862

Royal School of Needlework, 25 Princes Gate, London SW 7, England.

Mace and Nairn, 89 Crane Street, Salisbury, Wiltshire, England. Silk, cotton, gold and silver thread.

The Needlewoman Shop, 146 Regent Street, London W1, England. Linens, wool yarns, and cotton floss.

Alice Maynard, 724 Fifth Avenue, New York, N.Y. 10022.

A Schole-House for the Needle, Ltd., 1206 Jamestown Road, Williamsburg, Va. 23185. Canvas, silk mesh, Aida and Hardanger cloths, Paternayan Persian and crewel yarn, DMC cotton, silk and real gold and silver threads. Sample cards available.

Needle Arts, Inc., 2211 Monroe, Dearborn, Mich. 48124. Paternayan Persian yarn and Appleton tapestry yarn. Counted-thread-embroidery supplies.

Open Door to Stitchery, 4 Bond Street, Great Neck, N.Y. 11023. Paternayan Persian yarn.

*American Crewel and Canvas Studio, P.O. Box 298, Boonton, N.J. 07005. Unusual fabrics, silk thread, graph paper, even-weave fabrics.

Chaparral, 2505 River Oaks Boulevard, Houston, Texas 77019. Canvas, Aida and Hardanger cloths, Paternayan Persian and rug yarns, DMC cotton.

Keuffel and Esser Co., 40 East 43rd Street, New York, N.Y. 10017, or (for mail order) 20 Whippany Road, Morristown, N.J. 07960. Graph paper and drawing materials.

The Benevolent Elephant, 5 Broom House Road, London S.W.6, England. Paternayan Persian yarn.